PARKS & TRAILS NEW YORK

CYCLING THE HUDSON AND CHAMPLAIN VALLEYS

A GUIDE TO ART, HISTORY, AND NATURE ALONG THE NORTH-SOUTH ROUTE OF THE EMPIRE STATE TRAIL

T0287049

PARKS & TRAILS

NEW YORK

NEW YORK STATE OF OPPORTUNITY. | Hudson River Valley Greenway

Every effort has been made to make this guide as accurate and useful as possible. However, many things can change after publication – names of establishments, phone numbers, websites, and trail routing.

We encourage you to share your discoveries and insights along the way. Please submit comments and corrections by email to ptny@ptny.org.

ISBN 978-0-9748277-5-9
Printed in the United States
Copyright © 2022 Parks & Trails New York

Parks & Trails New York
33 Elk Street
Albany, NY 12207
www.ptny.org
ptny@ptny.org
518-434-1583

Use of this guide and its information are at the user's own risk.

Cyclists in Hudson Crossing Park

THIS PUBLICATION IS MADE POSSIBLE BY THE GENEROUS FINANCIAL SUPPORT OF THE FOLLOWING PARTNERS

Maurice D. Hinchey Hudson River Valley National Heritage Area

Hudson River Valley Greenway

Northern Border Regional Commission

Spring at the Walkway Over the Hudson

TABLE OF CONTENTS

TABLE OF CONTENTS

INTRODUCTION

Cycling the Hudson and Champlain Valleys follows the north-south section of the Hudson River Valley Greenway and Empire State Trail, from the southern tip of Manhattan in New York City to the Canada border at Rouses Point on the shores of Lake Champlain.

The Empire State Trail — the nation's longest multi-use state trail— spans 750 miles, from New York City through the Hudson and Champlain Valleys to Canada, and from Albany to Buffalo along the Erie Canal corridor. Statewide, 65 percent of the trail route is off-road; in the Hudson Valley 75 percent is off-road.

The Hudson River Valley Greenway — a unique state agency that preserves the scenic, natural, historic, cultural and recreational resources of the Hudson Valley — has been working since 1991 to establish a network of multi-use trails along the Hudson River. The Greenway is responsible for developing the 283-mile route from New York City to Whitehall, which is primarily an off-road trail. Whitehall marks the end of the Greenway trail, which continues north as an on-road bicycling route through the Champlain Valley to the Canada border. For more information on the Hudson River Valley Greenway, see hudsongreenway.ny.gov.

Users of this guidebook should consult the Empire State Trail website, empiretrail.ny.gov, for updates and links to information on temporary trail closures, detours, interactive online maps, and other trail information.

HOW TO USE THIS GUIDE

The *Cycling the Hudson and Champlain Valleys* guidebook is designed primarily for use by bicyclists, but it will also be useful to those enjoying the trail on foot, travelling waterways by boat, or for those visiting the area's many sites by car. It is divided into three primary sections: Overview, Maps, and Services. Information on cycling safety, travel, and logistics is also included.

Maps

The 44 full-color maps comprise the core of the guidebook. Four types of maps are included: overview, section, detail, and downtown inset. The map pages have colored borders, with the colors corresponding to one of four trail sections. For example, all the detail maps in the first section from New York City to Poughkeepsie have blue borders. Both the section and detail maps are numbered in ascending order from south to north. The pages opposite the maps contain information on points of interest and services.

Overview map

The overview map shows the location of the trail corridor within New York State relative to major geographic features and transportation gateways. It also depicts the coverage of the section maps.

Section maps

The four section maps show the location of the trail corridor relative to large- and moderate-size communities. They also depict the areas covered in the detail maps as numbered boxes. The section maps and their corresponding detail maps are color-coded as follows:

Section 1: New York City to Poughkeepsie

Section 2: Poughkeepsie to Albany

Section 3: Albany to Whitehall

Section 4: Whitehall to Rouses Point

Detail maps

Detail maps 4 to 25 cover an area of roughly 10 miles by 5 miles. Maps 1 to 3 cover smaller areas, roughly 3.5 miles by 1.75 miles, due to the concentration of attractions and services in Manhattan. Maps 26 to 30 cover larger areas, roughly 20 miles by 10 miles. Small diamonds along the frame of each detail map denote the scale.

Maps are centered along the trail corridor and identify trailhead and parking areas as well as points of interest and services. In addition, connector trails are highlighted for those who would like to take alternate routes. Available services in communities along the route are depicted with symbols on the page facing each detail map. The legend for the information displayed on the detail maps and facing pages can be found on the inside front cover.

Downtown insets

In the six major cities along the corridor, downtown inset maps are indicated by shaded boxes within the detail maps. The inset maps are labeled as 'A,' i.e. Map 10A.

Services

Lodging

This section contains information on the lodging options shown on the detail maps. Lodging facilities are grouped according to the detail map on which they appear, then by type of lodging: hotels or motels, and B&Bs, inns, cabins or hostels. Campgrounds are listed separately in the following section.

Bike shops

This section contains information on bike shops located within a reasonable ride of the Empire State Trail. Shops that offer bicycle rentals are indicated with asterisks.

Craft beverages

Wineries, breweries, and distilleries that are close to the route and have a tasting room, restaurant, or bar open to the public are listed in this section. The Hudson Valley has long been home to many wineries, and over the past decade New York State has seen a rapid growth of local breweries, cideries, and distilleries.

OVERVIEW

About the Empire State Trail

The north-south leg of the Empire State Trail route runs between New York City and the Canada border. The 283-mile Hudson River Valley Greenway Trail from Manhattan to Whitehall follows a number of rail-trails — examples include the Westchester South and North County Trails, the Maybrook Trailway, the Wallkill Valley Rail Trail, and the Albany-Hudson Electric Trail — each of which retains its local name and distinct character, co-branded as part of the larger Empire State Trail. From Waterford to Whitehall, the Hudson River Valley Greenway Trail follows the 75-mile Champlain Canalway Trail. North of Whitehall, the Empire State Trail runs 120 miles on road to Rouses Point, and should only be traveled by experienced cyclists comfortable riding on the shoulders of state highways with fast-moving and sometimes heavy traffic.

The Empire State Trail links major cities such as New York City, Poughkeepsie, Kingston, Albany, and Plattsburgh with smaller cities and villages such as New Paltz, Hudson, Troy, Schuylerville, Glens Falls, and Westport.

In the Albany area, the east-west leg of the Empire State Trail — the Erie Canalway Trail—splits from the north-south route and heads west to Buffalo. For more information on the east-west route of the Empire State Trail, visit empiretrail.ny.gov or cycletheeriecanal.com, or purchase *Cycling the Erie Canal*, a companion to this guidebook.

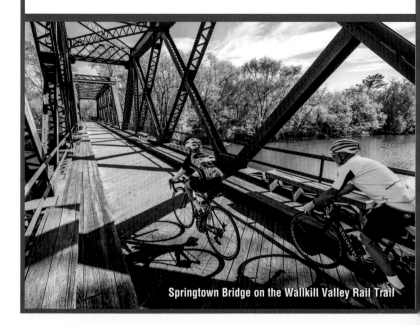

Springtown Bridge on the Wallkill Valley Rail Trail

Surface & grade

The Empire State Trail consists of both off-road and on-road components. Approximately 67% of the Hudson River Valley Greenway route between New York City and Whitehall is off-road, multi-use trail, comprised of 10-foot-wide improved trails with gentle grades, appropriate for riders of all ages and abilities.

The north-south leg of the Empire State Trail features three major surface conditions. Between Albany and New York City, the trail includes 127 miles of paved trail, 25 miles of stone dust trail, and 48 miles of on-road riding. From Albany north to Canada, the trail has 15 miles of paved trail and 14 miles of stone dust trail, nearly all of which is south of Whitehall, with the remaining 168 miles on road.

The stone dust trail sections are compacted, crushed limestone, which when dry is universally accessible and supports all types of bicycles. However, stonedust has greater rolling resistance than pavement and when wet can grab the narrow wheels of road bicycles and wheelchairs. Trail users should use caution under these conditions.

Paved sections of the off-road trail are generally asphalt, producing a ride experience similar to that found on the road.

The variety of surface conditions found along the trail means that a range of bicycle types can be used. Cyclists who prefer a more upright, relaxed riding style will be comfortable on hybrid or mountain bikes, although they may want to use non-knobby tires to improve efficiency over long distances. "Skinny-tire" road bikes can also be used, although some stretches of trail that have a stone dust surface will be somewhat challenging on tires that are less than 30 mm in width. The wider tires and tire clearance found on touring or gravel bikes are ideal for trail use.

Getting to the trail

Visitors can reach the Hudson and Champlain corridor by several means of transportation. Check the section overviews for more regional transportation information.

Train

Sixteen Amtrak stations provide rail service along the route, generally running parallel to the Hudson River and Lake Champlain. Multiple trains serve stations between New York City and Albany each day, but only one daily train in each direction continues on to Montreal. Amtrak's bicycle transport options are included in the Travel & Logistics section.

Bus

Long-distance bus lines serve most of the larger cities along the southern half of the route between New York City and Albany, with Greyhound and Trailways the two main ticketing companies. Transporting a full-size bicycle by bus almost always requires breaking down the bicycle to fit in a standard shipping box, or "boxing" it. See the Travel & Logistics section for more information.

Auto

The New York State Thruway (I-87), and the Taconic State Parkway, a scenic byway, roughly parallel the trail and are the primary arteries for automotive travel through the Hudson Valley.

The Empire State Trail is, for the most part, easy to access as there are numerous trailheads with formalized parking spaces. Trailheads with parking areas are shown on the detail maps.

Downtown areas of cities and villages usually have designated parking areas. However, these areas are frequently limited to short-term parking. Be sure to check the posted parking regulations before setting out on an overnight trip. In large cities, paid parking lots close to the trail route are often the most convenient and secure options; consult a visitor's center or the tourism promotion agency for that region for more information. If you plan to stay overnight at hotels or B&B's, you might also ask to use their parking facilities.

Riders at an informational kiosk in Manhattan

Transit

New York City is served by an extensive subway system. Much of the southernmost portion of the Empire State Trail is within a few blocks of a subway line. Stations along the 1, 7, A, C, or E line provide the easiest access. Check ahead for MTA restrictions, however most subway lines allow passengers to take bicycles on board. New York City and other larger urban and suburban areas also have regional bus service that can be used to reach trail access points, with many buses equipped to carry bicycles. Contact information for regional transit systems is listed on the introductory page for each of the four guidebook sections.

Weather

For cyclists and walkers, May through September offers the best weather for an extended trip on the Empire State Trail. June, July, and August tend to be the sunniest and driest months. Summer precipitation often means short but powerful thunderstorms with heavy rain. Spring and fall rain showers tend to be lighter, but last longer.

Between Glens Falls and Plattsburgh, on the northern sections of the trail, weather is more variable due to the adjacent Adirondack mountains. Summers in the Adirondacks are moderately warm and humid, while winters can be very cold. Spring and fall seasons are variable, and tend towards greater amounts of precipitation. Snowy conditions can occur between October and May, with the greatest likelihood of steady snow between December and March. In spite of frequent precipitation, the Adirondacks enjoy many sunny days in the summertime. The nearby Adirondack mountains and wide expanse of Lake Champlain often results in windy conditions.

For weather conditions and forecasts, visit the National Weather Service homepage (weather.gov) and look up the weather for the cities and towns you will be passing through.

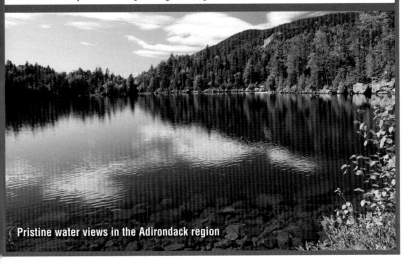

Pristine water views in the Adirondack region

Multi-day trips

This guidebook is particularly useful for those planning multi-day trips or traveling the entire north-south length of the Empire State Trail.

While each bicyclist travels at his/her/their own pace, recreational cyclists typically cover 30 to 50 miles per day. An average of approximately 40 miles per day allows significant daily progress while ensuring time to visit many of the interesting sites along the route. At this pace, it takes roughly 10 days to travel the 400-mile route from New York City to the Canada border. For cyclists who don't have the time to ride the entire trail in one trip, or who prefer to remain on the primarily off-road pathways between New York City and Whitehall, the guidebook has been divided into four sections. Sections 1 through 3 (NYC to Albany to Whitehall) are primarily off-road, non-motorized trails, with some connecting on-road segments. The northern-most Section 4, from Whitehall to Rouses Point, is almost entirely on-road cycling on state highways. Each section is between 75 to 125 miles long, a length that can easily be cycled over the course of a long weekend, including travel time to and from the trail.

Camping accommodations along the trail

Camping opportunities in the Hudson Valley between NYC and Albany are limited near the trail. A greater number of public and private campgrounds are available along the Champlain corridor. See section maps for campground locations. Contact information for all campgrounds can be found in the Lodging section.

Primitive camping is allowed along the Champlain Canalway Trail at locks C4 and C9. These primitive campsites have limited on-site amenities. Porta johns are provided, but visitors should be prepared with their own potable water, first aid kits, and camping and cooking supplies. Stays are limited to 48 hours and are available on a first come first serve basis. Campers should provide advance notice by contacting the sites at the phone numbers listed on page 122. Please note that, other than along the Canal locks, primitive camping is not available directly on the Empire State Trail.

Other accommodations

Another opportunity for overnight accommodations along the Empire State Trail is through Warmshowers, a worldwide hospitality exchange for touring cyclists. Visit warmshowers.org for more information.

For those seeking formal lodging, the guidebook identifies many inns, bed & breakfasts, and traditional hotels and motels near the route.

A brief history of the Hudson and Champlain Valleys

The Hudson and Champlain Valleys are among the most iconic and beautiful, historically important, and evocative locations in the United States and are an enduring part of our natural and cultural heritage.

Doorways and Passages

Indigenous peoples inhabited the Hudson River and Lake Champlain for thousands of years before European colonization. Prior to 1609, the river was known as the Muhheakunnuk by the Lenape, meaning "river that flows both ways," and the lake was called 'Kaniá:tare tsi kahnhokà:ronte' by the Mohawk, meaning "door of the country" or "doorway lake." Both waterways and their tributaries have been a life-giving source of food, fresh water, irrigation, and a means for travel and trade. After European explorers arrived in 1609 and recounted the rich natural resources they encountered, Dutch and British settlers flocked to the "New World" to seek their fortunes, at the expense and violent displacement of Native Americans. European colonists often named places derived from the Native languages of those who inhabited the land before, including Manhattan, Mahopac, Poughkeepsie, Cohoes, and the Adirondacks, to name a few.

More than 150 years after colonization, the Hudson and Champlain Valleys were the settings for some of the most strategically decisive battles of the Revolutionary War. The region's natural beauty inspired the first truly American painters and writers. See the Hudson River Art Trail at hudsonriverschool.org for more information. Innovation led to the development of industry and a network of cities. Important social reforms such as abolition, women's rights, and organized labor took hold here. For a more complete history, the region is home to three National Heritage Areas: the Maurice D. Hinchey Hudson River Valley National Heritage Area (hudsonrivervalley.com), the Champlain Valley National Heritage Partnership (champlainvalleynhp.org) and the Erie Canalway National Heritage Corridor (eriecanalway.org).

The population of both the Hudson Valley and the Lake Champlain Basin has increased in the 21st century, as the natural beauty, rich history, and modern amenities of the area have drawn urban and rural dwellers. Environmental protection has become a key issue, highlighting the importance of sustainable growth and responding to climate change.

Whether captivated by majestic vistas, the allure of quaint villages, the pleasures of walking and biking on tree-lined trails, or the connection with nature and the past available at many parks and historic sites, the region continues to capture the hearts and minds of residents and visitors alike.

Natural Resources

The Hudson River Valley was sculpted by the advance and retreat of glacial ice sheets during the last Ice Age, approximately 25,000 years ago. The river's course runs 315 miles from its source at Lake Tear of the Clouds in the Adirondacks to the Battery at the tip of Manhattan. The estuary—the part of the river affected by tides—is 158 miles from Troy to New York Harbor. As the river travels with the tide, rising towards Troy or flowing south towards the sea, the sea water becomes diluted with fresh water runoff. This mineral-rich water creates a bountiful ecosystem, with 200+ species of fish, birds such as eagles, osprey, herons and waterfowl, and more than a dozen oak, hickory, and willow species. It is no wonder that when European explorers arrived at the Hudson River they found thousands of Native people inhabiting its valley.

Northward, the Champlain Valley, which extends from Whitehall to southern Québec, was also shaped by glacial movement. The melting of the last glaciers created the Champlain Sea, a vast inlet connecting the Atlantic Ocean to the St. Lawrence River. The land slowly rose in elevation over thousands of years, and the sea retreated to become what is now Lake Champlain. The fossils of whales, walruses, seals, ocean fish, and clams have been found around Montreal and Ottawa, inhabitants of the former saltwater inlet. The unique geological history of the Lake Champlain Basin created a special ecosystem that has survived for millennia, recognized in 1989 by UNESCO as a Biosphere Reserve site, in combination with the neighboring Adirondack Mountains. The biosphere is the largest protected area in the eastern United States, and is home to thousands of animal and plant species, dozens of which are exclusive to the lake.

Indigenous Land

Both the Hudson and Champlain Valleys were populated by Indigenous peoples, including the Wappinger, Lenape, Mohican, Mohawk, Abenaki, and Haudenosaunee. These groups shared overlapping territories throughout New York, and most looked to waterways for sustenance and transportation. Artifacts have been discovered along the Hudson River and in the Adirondack-Champlain region dating back 7,000 to 10,000 years.

European Colonization and Immigration

European explorers viewed land and water as opportunities for profit and exploitation. The first known European to travel to the Hudson River was Giovanni da Verrazano, in 1524. In 1609, the Dutch East India Company hired Henry Hudson to find a passage from the river to China. In the same year, Samuel de Champlain, a French navigator traveling in the territory he called Québec, heard from Native people of a large lake to the south, surrounded by beautiful mountains. Upon finding the lake, Champlain named it after himself.

After initial exploration and "discovery," European settlements grew into established trading posts. The resultant thriving trade turned the Hudson River into a major transportation corridor. Similarly, Lake Champlain developed into a water and ice passage between the Saint Lawrence and Hudson Rivers. The French built several forts to try to control the flow of travelers and trade along the Champlain passageway. All of these efforts came at the expense of Native peoples, whose land was taken in the decades after colonization.

Historic Battlegrounds

The Hudson River and Lake Champlain regions played an outsized role in the struggle for American independence. Moving down from Canada and up from Long Island and New York City, the British forces tried desperately to control the river, which was a major supply route for the American armies, and to sever New England from the rest of the colonies. Kingston, then the New York State capital, was burned to the ground, the American Navy was established at Whitehall, and battles were fought at Saratoga, Ticonderoga, Crown Point, and Valcour Island. Later in American history, one of the key battles of the War of 1812 took place in Plattsburgh. The battle of Saratoga was the turning point in the Revolution and Saratoga National Historic Park is along the trail route in Section 3. Rogers Island, just south of Glens Falls, was a sporadic military encampment and training site from the French and Indian War to the Civil War.

Industrial Connections

The Hudson River Valley was of strategic importance during the Industrial Revolution. Foundries, quarries, textile mills, coal yards, brickyards and other industrial sites flourished in the valley, powered by waterfalls on the river's tributaries and using the well-established transportation system along the river itself. The invention of the steamboat in 1807 speeded travel up and down the river.

Until this time, trade and travel between the Champlain and Hudson Valleys posed a challenge due to lengthy overland portages between the two water bodies. The opening in 1823 of the Champlain Canal, which ran from Cohoes to Whitehall and connected the two valleys, and the development of the better known Erie Canal, opened in 1825, led to the Hudson River becoming the critical link between New York City and all points north and west in the growing United States. As railways sprung up across New York State later in the century, both goods and passengers could travel more efficiently from New York harbor up the river and across the country.

A Tide of Tourists, Artists, and Writers

Steamboats and railroads opened the Hudson and Champlain Valleys to tourism as well as industry. In the nineteenth century, visitors flocked to Upstate New York, charmed by its natural beauty and abundant resources. During the Gilded Age, many New York City industrialists and financiers built large country homes along the Hudson River and camps in the Adirondacks. Resorts and summer vacation rentals flourished around Lake Champlain and in the Catskills.

The dramatic beauty of the Hudson River inspired its own art movement, known as the Hudson River School. Thomas Cole, Frederic Church, Jasper Cropsey, and Asher Durand painted and popularized sublime and picturesque vistas of the valley. Similarly, Lake Champlain's stunning mountain views were a muse for Winslow Homer, Andrew Wyeth, Maxfield Parrish, and Ogden Pleissner. Many famous writers, including Washington Irving, James Fenimore Cooper, Herman Melville and, later, Edna St. Vincent Millay and John Cheever, also flocked to the region and incorporated the locales into their works.

Activism and the Flow of Ideas

New York State played a significant role in the history of the abolition of slavery, the fight for women's suffrage, and the labor movement. Many of the famous people who contributed to these fights for human progress lived and worked in the cities and towns along the Empire State Trail. The Underground Railroad, a secret network of housing, resources, and trustworthy contacts, moved formerly enslaved persons to safety and freedom through Upstate to Canada. Across New York, women suffragists agitated for the right to vote, and ultimately shaped the national conversation on the then-controversial issue. After the Industrial Revolution and the rise of "robber baron" industrialists, workers in New York began organizing for fairer pay, safer labor conditions, and better working hours.

PRONUNCIATION GUIDE

Rouses Point	Rou-ziz Point
Chazy	Chay-zee
Ticonderoga	Tie-con-der-oh-gah
Schuylerville	Sky-ler-ville
Cohoes	Kuh-hose
Albany	All-buh-knee
Rensselaer	Ren-suh-leer
Valatie	Vuh-lay-shuh
Linlithgo	Luhn-lith-go
Tivoli	Ti-vuh-lee
Poughkeepsie	Puh-kip-see
Mahopac	May-uh-pak

Common Ground

Industrialization and rising populations brought pollution and environmental degradation to both valleys, becoming more pronounced in the twentieth century. Environmental movements have since responded to educate the public and change local, state, and national laws to protect New York's water, air, and land. Protecting the environment remains a crucial concern to combat climate change and to serve the best interests of future generations.

Early conservationists understood that it would take a concerted effort to defend the natural beauty and historic character of the Hudson River Valley. One tactic has been the donation of private land into public trusts. Mary Harriman, George W. Perkins, and members of the Rockefeller family, among others, gave thousands of acres of land to create state parks and historic sites for public use and enjoyment.

In 1989, UNESCO recognized the Lake Champlain Basin and Adirondack region as a key area for conservation and created the Champlain-Adirondack Biosphere Network, a protected biosphere reserve. Around the same time, the work of local and regional activists and elected officials led to state legislation creating the Hudson River Valley Greenway in 1991 and the passage of federal legislation creating the Maurice D. Hinchey Hudson River Valley National Heritage Area in 1996 to preserve, protect, and celebrate the area's cultural and natural resources.

Empire State Trail

In January 2017, New York State announced the creation of the Empire State Trail, a 750-mile bicycle and walking trail that spans New York State from New York City to Canada and from Albany to Buffalo. The project incorporated existing trails and provided $200 million for the construction of new trail segments to connect and enhance existing trails. Wayfinding signage for the Empire State Trail can be found along the entire length of the route, along with improved gateways and access points that include parking facilities, welcome and orientation signage, picnic tables and benches, and bicycle racks and self-service bicycle "fix-it" stations.

Looking Ahead

Appreciation of the Hudson and Champlain Valleys continues to grow as communities reconnect to the land, the waterfront, and their history. Use of public lands and trails is increasing, and interest in the region's historic heritage endures. Local and state groups recognize the importance of telling New York's stories through a wider cultural lens, and re-examining the narratives that have led us to the present, in the hope of attaining a more equitable, green, and promising future for all.

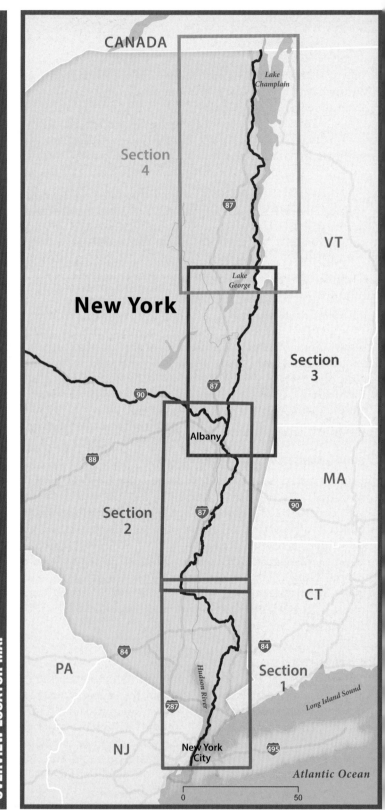

ROUTE MILEAGE

Total	New York City to Canada Border	400 miles	
Section 1	New York City to Poughkeepsie	102 miles	Maps 1 to 10A
Section 2	Poughkeepsie to Albany	99 miles	Maps 11 to 17
Section 3	Albany to Whitehall	76 miles	Maps 18 to 25
Section 4	Whitehall to Rouses Point	123 miles	Maps 25 to 30

STATE TOURISM INFORMATION

I Love NY	iloveny.com	(800) CALL-NYS

ADDITIONAL CYCLING INFORMATION

Empire State Trail	empiretrail.ny.gov	
Parks & Trails New York	ptny.org	(518) 434-1583
NYS Department of Transportation	dot.ny.gov/bicycle	(518) 457-6195

MAJOR CITIES BY POPULATION (2020 DATA)

New York City	8,804,190	Albany	99,224
Yonkers	211,569	Troy	51,401
Poughkeepsie	31,577	Cohoes	18,147
Kingston	24,069	Mechanicville	5,163
Hudson	5,894	Glens Falls	14,830

HISTORICAL INFORMATION

Hudson River Valley National Heritage Area	hudsonrivervalley.com	(518) 473-3835
Champlain Valley National Heritage Partnership	champlainvalleynhp.org	(800) 468-5227
Erie Canalway National Heritage Corridor	eriecanalway.org	(518) 237-7000
New York Heritage Digital Collections	nyheritage.org	
New York State Museum	nysm.nysed.gov	(518) 474-5877

TRAVEL INFORMATION

Train Lines

Amtrak	amtrak.com	(800) USA-RAIL
Metro-North	new.mta.info	(212) 532-4900
VIA Rail Canada	viarail.ca	(888) VIA-RAIL

Bus Lines

Greyhound	greyhound.com	(800) 231-2222
Trailways	trailways.com	(800) 858-8555
Megabus	us.megabus.com	(877) GO2-MEGA
OurBus	ourbus.com	(844) 800-6828

Automobile

New York State Thruway	thruway.ny.gov	(800) THRUWAY

Commercial Airports

LaGuardia International Airport (LGA)	laguardiaairport.com	(718) 533-3400
John F. Kennedy International Airport (JFK)	jfkairport.com	(718) 244-4444
New York Stewart International Airport (SWF)	swfny.com	(845) 838-8200
Newark Liberty International Airport (EWR)	newarkairport.com	(973) 961-6000
Albany International (ALB)	albanyairport.com	(518) 242-2000
Plattsburgh International Airport (PBG)	flyplattsburgh.com	(518) 565-4795

N

44
9
44
10A Downtown Poughkeepsie
Dutchess Co.
10 Poughkeepsie
Ulster Co.
87
9 Hopewell Junction
9W
84
9
8 Brewster
Putnam Co.
Orange Co.
86
7 Mahopac - Carmel
6
87
6 Briarcliff Manor - Yorktown Heights
Westchester Co.
684
9W
Rockland Co.
Connecticut
287
5 Ardsley - Pleasantville
9
95
New Jersey
87
4 Bronx - Yonkers
2 Midtown West - Upper West Side
3 West Harlem
25A
295
495
1 Lower Manhattan - Greenwich Village

0   10

SECTION 1
NEW YORK CITY TO POUGHKEEPSIE

The southern half of the Hudson Valley Greenway Trail connects New York City to Poughkeepsie. This 102-mile stretch consists of Manhattan's Hudson River Greenway Trail, the Westchester South and North County Trails, the Putnam Trailway, the Maybrook Trailway, and the William R. Steinhaus Dutchess Rail Trail, along with a few short-distance on-road connections between these trails.

The Empire State Trail's southernmost point is at the intersection of Battery Place and West Street in Lower Manhattan, and the trail runs north through Battery Park City and Hudson River Park along the island's west side. The most heavily used greenway trail in the United States, the Hudson River Greenway is popular with cyclists, pedestrians, and skaters. Riders should ride slowly, be prepared for crossing traffic, and expect to share the lane with others. At West 59th Street, the trail enters Riverside Park and continues north, providing dramatic views of the New York City skyline, the Hudson River, and the George Washington Bridge.

From Dyckman Street in northwest Manhattan to Van Cortlandt Park in the Bronx, riders must use a 3-mile on-road segment through city neighborhoods. This on-road section, which is appropriate for experienced bicyclists comfortable riding next to vehicle traffic and parked cars, follows a designated NYC bicycle route but does not have a protected bike lane. The route crosses Broadway Bridge to pass from Manhattan to the Bronx. On this bridge, bicyclists can ride across with traffic, or dismount and walk on the bridge's sidewalks.

In Van Cortlandt Park, the trail route is once again off-road, and is known as the Putnam Greenway within the park. From Van Cortlandt Park north to Brewster in Putnam County, the Hudson River Valley Greenway Trail follows an entirely off-road rail trail. The trail runs along the South County Trail and North County Trail in Westchester County. Elmsford marks the break between the south and north portions of the trail. From the Putnam County line north, near Mahopac, the route moves on to the Putnam Trailway. These four segments – the Putnam Greenway, the Westchester South and North County Trails, and the Putnam Trailway – function as a continuous 48-mile trail, all following the same old rail bed.

At the north end of the Putnam Trailway, a short 1-mile on-road section in the village of Brewster connects to the Maybrook Trailway. Visitor amenities are available in Brewster – north of Brewster, there are few public services near the trail for the next 24 miles, until reaching Hopewell Junction in Dutchess County. Riders should plan accordingly.

At Hopewell Junction, the route moves on to the William R. Steinhaus Dutchess Rail Trail for the final 13.5 miles to Poughkeepsie.

COMMUNITIES ALONG ROUTE

New York County	Lower Manhattan, Greenwich Village, Midtown, Upper West Side, Harlem
Bronx County	The Bronx
Westchester County	Yonkers, Ardsley, Elmsford, Hawthorne, Briarcliff Manor, Yorktown Heights
Putnam County	Mahopac, Carmel, Brewster
Dutchess County	Hopewell Junction, Poughkeepsie

VISITOR INFORMATION

New York County	nycgo.com	(800) NYC-VISIT
Bronx County	nycgo.com	(800) NYC-VISIT
Westchester County	visitwestchesterny.com	(914) 995-8500
Putnam County	putnamcountyny.com	(845) 808-1015
Dutchess County	dutchesstourism.com	(845) 463-4000

SAFETY & SECURITY

Universal Emergency Number: 911

Law Enforcement

State Police Troop NYC	Bronx, Kings, New York, Queens, Richmond Counties	(212) 459-7800
State Police Troop K	Westchester, Putnam, Dutchess Counties	(845) 677-7300
NYPD	All Boroughs	(646) 610-5000
Westchester County Public Safety	Hawthorne	(914) 864-7700
Putnam County Sheriff's Dept.	Carmel	(845) 225-4300
Dutchess County Sheriff's Dept.	Poughkeepsie	(845) 486-3800

Cyclists on the Hudson River Greenway

TRANSPORTATION

Rail Service
Amtrak (Intercity Rail)   amtrak.com   (800) USA-RAIL
Metro-North (Commuter Rail)   new.mta.info   (212) 532-4900

Major Rail Stations
New York-Penn Station   2 Pennsylvania Plaza
  (Amtrak, LIRR, NJ Transit)
New York-Grand Central (Metro-North)   89 E 42nd St.
Yonkers (Amtrak, Metro-North)   5 Buena Vista Ave.
Brewster (Metro-North)   9 Main St.
Poughkeepsie (Amtrak, Metro-North)   41 Main St.

Major Bus Stations
Port Authority Bus Terminal   625 8th Ave.   (212) 564-8484

Urban & Regional Transit
MTA Subway   new.mta.info
MTA Bus   new.mta.info
MTA Metro-North   new.mta.info
Westchester County Bee-Line Bus   transportation.westchestergov.com/bee-line
Megabus   us.megabus.com
Adirondack Trailways   trailways.com

Commercial Airports
LaGuardia International Airport (LGA)   laguardiaairport.com
John F. Kennedy International Airport (JFK) jfkairport.com
New York Stewart International Airport (SWF) swfny.com
Newark Liberty International Airport (EWR) newarkairport.com

HOSPITALS

Bellevue Hospital Center - New York   (212) 562-5555
Harlem Hospital Center - New York   (212) 939-1000
Lenox Hill Hospital - New York   (212) 434-2000
Metropolitan Hospital Center - New York   (212) 423-6262
Mount Sinai Beth Israel - New York   (212) 857-9980
Mount Sinai West - New York   (212) 523-4000
New York-Presbyterian Hospital - New York   (212) 932-4000
NYU Langone Tisch Hospital - New York   (212) 263-6906
Phelps Hospital - Tarrytown   (914) 366-3000
Putnam Hospital Center - Carmel   (845) 302-3491
St. John's Riverside Hospital -Yonkers   (914) 964-4444
St. Joseph's Medical Center - Yonkers   (914) 378-7000
Vassar Brothers Medical Center - Poughkeepsie   (845) 454-8500

The William R. Steinhaus Dutchess Rail Trail

MAP 1 LOWER MANHATTAN - GREENWICH VILLAGE

1 MILE

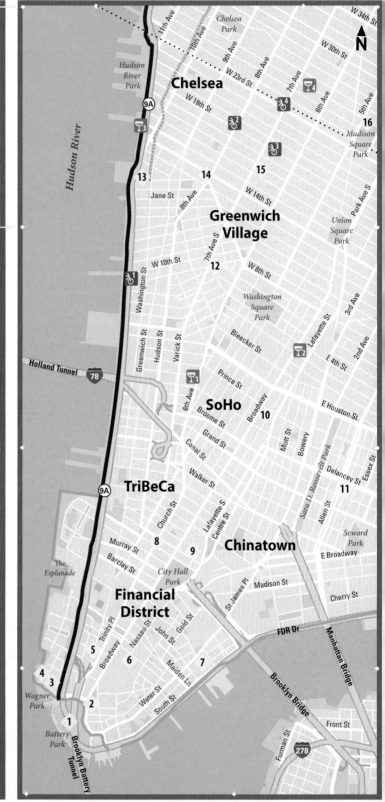

THINGS TO SEE & DO

#			
1.	Castle Clinton National Monument	Battery Park	(212) 344-7220
2.	National Museum of the American Indian	1 Bowling Green	(212) 514-3700
3.	The Skyscraper Museum	39 Battery Pl.	(212) 945-6324
4.	Museum of Jewish Heritage	36 Battery Pl.	(646) 437-4202
5.	9/11 Memorial & Tribute Museum	92 Greenwich St.	(212) 422-3520
6.	Federal Hall National Memorial	26 Wall St.	(212) 825-6990
7.	South Street Seaport District & Museum	19 Fulton St.	(212) 748-8600
8.	The Oculus	50 Church St.	
9.	African Burial Ground National Monument	290 Broadway	(212) 238-4367
10.	Museum of Ice Cream	558 Broadway	
11.	Tenement Museum	103 Orchard St.	(877) 975-3786
12.	Stonewall National Monument	38-64 Christopher St.	(212) 668-2577
13.	Whitney Museum of American Art	99 Gansevoort St.	(212) 570-3600
14.	Museum of Illusions	77 8th Ave.	(212) 645-3230
15.	Rubin Museum of Art	150 W 17th St.	(212) 620-5000
16.	National Museum of Mathematics	11 E 26th St.	(212) 542-0566

TRAIL & TRAVEL NOTES

The Battery — The off-road Hudson River Greenway Trail begins in The Battery, a city park at the southernmost tip of Manhattan. The Battery features beautiful views of New York Harbor and the Statue of Liberty, and is home to the Castle Clinton National Monument. Castle Clinton, built in 1811, has operated as a military fort, an entertainment venue, New York's first immigration processing center, and the original home of the New York City Aquarium.

VISITOR INFORMATION

NYC Go
(800) NYC-VISIT
nycgo.com

AMENITIES

Manhattan

Illustration of Castle Clinton, circa 1892

THE PORT OF NEW YORK.

View of Lower Manhattan
from New York Harbor

N

Riverside Park

W 91st St

Broadway

Amsterdam Ave

W 86th St

West End Ave

Jacqueline Kennedy Onassis Reservoir

18

E 86th St

Upper West Side

W 81st St

Theodore Roosevelt Park

Central Park

17

W 79th St

16

E 79th St

Columbus Ave

W 76th St

15

Madison Ave

The Lake

W 72nd St 4

5

E 72nd St

Hudson River

9A

W 66th St

Central Park West

5th Ave

E 66th St

Riverside Park South

3

Amsterdam Ave

13

Broadway

14

Park Ave

West End Ave

The Pond

E 60th St

Central Park South

MANHATTAN GREENWAY TRAIL

W 57th St

12

E 57th St

DeWitt Clinton Park

W 54th St

W 53rd St

11

E 53rd St

9th Ave

8th Ave

7th Ave

9

6th Ave

10

5th Ave

E 50th St

11th Ave

10th Ave

W 49th St

W 45th St

8

2

W 42nd St

Midtown

E 46th St

MTA

7

E 42nd St

Hell's Kitchen

5

Bryant Park 6

Madison Ave

Lincoln Tunnel

495

W 37th St

W 36th St

E 37th St

W 34th St

?

E 34th St

4

1

W 33rd St

2

3

E 30th St

9A

1

Chelsea Park

5th Ave

Park Ave S

Chelsea

11th Ave

10th Ave

W 23rd St

8th Ave

7th Ave

6th Ave

Madison Square Park

THINGS TO SEE & DO

#			
1.	The High Line	Gansevoort St. to W 30th St.	(212) 500-6035
2.	Madison Square Garden	4 Pennsylvania Plz.	(212) 465-6000
3.	Empire State Building	20 W 34th St.	(212) 736-3100
4.	Hudson Yards	Hudson Yards	(646) 954-3155
5.	Times Square	42nd St. & 8th Ave.	(212) 768-1560
6.	New York Public Library	476 5th Ave.	(917) 275-6975
7.	Grand Central Terminal	89 E 42nd St.	(212) 340-2583
8.	Intrepid Sea, Air, & Space Museum	Pier 86, W 46th St.	(212) 245-0072
9.	St. Patrick's Cathedral	14 E 51st St.	(212) 753-2261
10.	Rockefeller Center	45 Rockefeller Plz.	(212) 588-8601
11.	Museum of Modern Art - MoMA	11 W 53rd St.	(212) 708-9400
12.	Carnegie Hall	881 7th Ave.	(212) 247-7800
13.	Lincoln Center for the Performing Arts	Lincoln Center Plz.	(212) 875-5456
14.	Central Park Zoo	E 64th St. & 5th Ave.	(212) 439-6500
15.	New-York Historical Society	170 Central Park W	(212) 873-3400
16.	American Museum of Natural History	200 Central Park W	(212) 769-5100
17.	Metropolitan Museum of Art	1000 5th Ave.	(212) 535-7710
18.	Solomon R. Guggenheim Museum	1071 5th Ave.	(212) 423-3500

TRAIL & TRAVEL NOTES

Central Park — Visited annually by over 42 million people, Central Park is one of the most famous public spaces in the world. Designed by famed landscape architects Frederick Law Olmsted and Calvert Vaux, the 843-acre park incudes several man-made lakes and ponds, picturesque bridges and arches, monuments, playgrounds, foundations, and a large reservoir, outdoor ampitheater, swimming pool, ice-skating rink, zoo, carousel and a castle. The park was completed in 1876, but rock outcroppings and boulders on the grounds date back 190 million to 1.1 billion years, and feature markings from glacial movement during the last ice age.

VISITOR INFORMATION

NYC Go
151 W 34th St.
(800) NYC-VISIT
nycgo.com

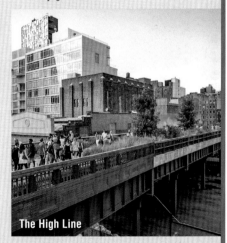

The High Line

Fall colors in Central Park

1 MILE

MAP 3   WEST HARLEM

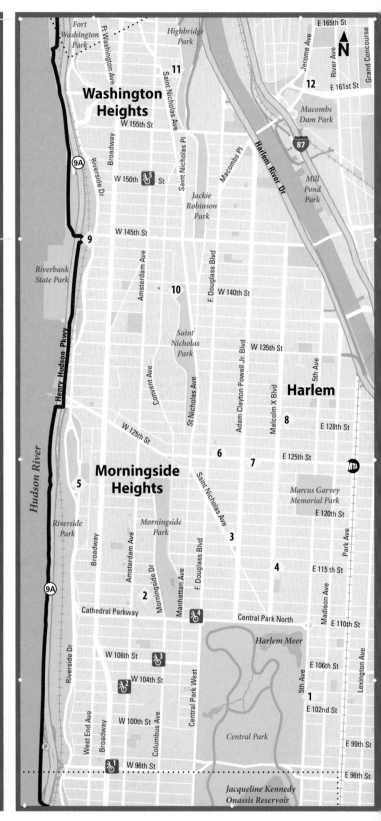

N

Fort Washington Park

Highbridge Park

E 165th St

Jerome Ave

River Ave

Grand Concourse

E 161st St

Washington Heights

W 155th St

11

12

Macombs Dam Park

I-87

Mill Pond Park

9A

Riverside Dr

Broadway

W 150th St

5

Saint Nicholas Ave

Saint Nicholas Pl

Macombs Pl

Harlem River Dr

W 145th St

9

Jackie Robinson Park

Riverbank State Park

Amsterdam Ave

10

F. Douglass Blvd

W 140th St

W 135th St

Adam Clayton Powell Jr. Blvd

Malcolm X Blvd

5th Ave

Harlem

Saint Nicholas Park

Henry Hudson Pkwy

Convent Ave

St Nicholas Ave

W 125th St

8

E 128th St

E 125th St

MTA

Hudson River

5

6

7

Morningside Heights

Saint Nicholas Ave

Marcus Garvey Memorial Park

E 120th St

Riverside Park

Broadway

Amsterdam Ave

Morningside Park

Morningside Dr

Manhattan Ave

F. Douglass Blvd

3

4

E 115th St

Park Ave

9A

2

Cathedral Parkway

4

Central Park North

E 110th St

Madison Ave

Harlem Meer

E 106th St

W 106th St

3

W 104th St

2

West End Ave

Broadway

Columbus Ave

Central Park West

5th Ave

Lexington Ave

1

W 100th St

P

W 96th St

1

E 102nd St

E 99th St

Central Park

E 96th St

Jacqueline Kennedy Onassis Reservoir

THINGS TO SEE & DO

1.	Museum of the City of New York	1220 5th Ave.	(212) 534-1672
2.	Cathedral Church of St. John the Divine	1047 Amsterdam Ave.	(212) 316-7540
3.	Minton's Playhouse	206 W 118th St.	(212) 243-2222
4.	Harlem Heritage Tourism and Cultural Center	104 Malcolm X Blvd.	(212) 280-7888
5.	General Grant National Memorial	W 122nd St. & Riverside Dr.	(646) 670-7251
6.	Apollo Theater	253 W 125th St.	(212) 531-5300
7.	The Studio Museum in Harlem	144 W 125th St.	(212) 864-4500
8.	National Jazz Museum in Harlem	58 W 129th St.	(212) 348-8300
9.	Riverbank State Park	679 Riverside Dr.	(212) 694-3600
10.	Hamilton Grange	414 W 141st St.	(646) 548-2310
11.	Morris-Jumel Mansion	65 Jumel Terr.	(212) 923-8008
12.	Yankee Stadium	1 E 161st St.	(212) 926-5337

TRAIL & TRAVEL NOTES

Harlem's Cultural Heritage — Harlem, named by Dutch colonists after a city in the Netherlands, was originally a hunting ground for the Weckquaesgeek, part of the Wappinger people. Harlem developed over time from open flatlands to farming country, then into mixed residential and industrial usage. In the 1920s, a highly influential cultural revolution, known as the Harlem Renaissance, began in the neighborhood. Langston Hughes, Zora Neale Hurston, Louis Armstrong, and Marcus Garvey were a few of the many Black writers, artists, and innovators who lived in Harlem at that time and contributed to the historic period.

"Time in this place does not obey an order" — wrote Jorge Luis Borges in his poem, "The Cloisters." Constructed from the remains of five French abbeys, the Met Cloisters (part of the Metropolitan Museum of Art) transports visitors to Medieval Europe. The museum contains over 3,000 works of art dating as far back as the ninth century.

VISITOR INFORMATION

NYC Go
(800) NYC-VISIT
nycgo.com

Zora Neale Hurtson, pre-eminent Black writer

Sunset on the Greenway Trail on the west side of Manhattan

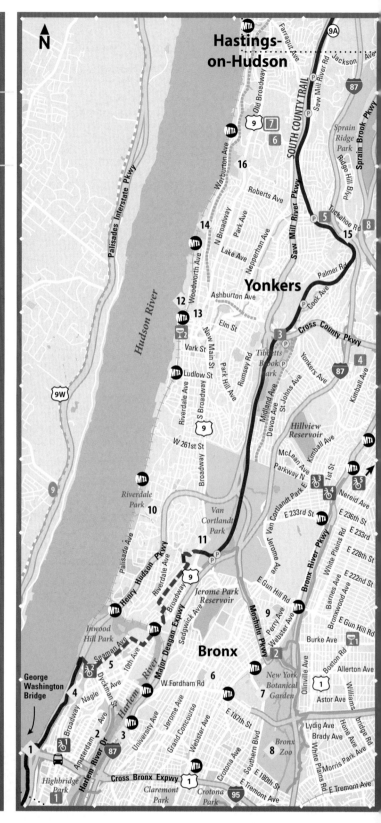

1 MILE

MAP 4   BRONX - YONKERS

THINGS TO SEE & DO

1.	The Little Red Lighthouse	Fort Washington Park	(212) 628-2345
2.	The High Bridge	W 172nd St. & Amsterdam Ave.	(212) 639-9675
3.	Roberto Clemente State Park	301 W Tremont Ave.	(718) 299-8750
4.	The Met Cloisters	99 Margaret Corbin Dr.	(212) 923-3700
5.	Dyckman Farmhouse Museum	4881 Broadway	(212) 304-9422
6.	Edgar Allen Poe Cottage	2640 Grand Concourse	(718) 881-8900
7.	New York Botanical Garden	2900 Southern Blvd.	(718) 817-8700
8.	Bronx Zoo	2300 Southern Blvd.	(718) 220-5100
9.	Museum of Bronx History	3266 Bainbridge Ave.	(718) 881-8900
10.	Wave Hill Garden & Cultural Center	4900 Independence Ave.	(718) 549-3200
11.	Van Cortlandt House Museum	6035 Broadway	(718) 543-3344
12.	Groundwork Hudson Valley Science Barge	99 Dock St.	(914) 375-2151
13.	Philipse Manor Hall State Historic Site	29 Warburton Ave.	(914) 965-4027
14.	Hudson River Museum	511 Warburton Ave.	(914) 963-4550
15.	Historic Sherwood House	340 Tuckahoe Rd.	(914) 961-8940
16.	Untermyer Gardens	945 N Broadway	(914) 613-4502

TRAIL & TRAVEL NOTES

Gorgeous Gardens — The Bronx's impressive outdoor sites offer a chance to escape from the bustle of the city. The New York Botanical Garden features over one million plants, including a 50-acre section of old-growth forest that has never been logged. The Peggy Rockefeller Rose Garden, part of the botanical garden, includes over 650 varieties of roses in bloom from May to October—an incredible sensory experience for those who enjoy the scent of flowers. Wave Hill is a 28-acre estate featuring outdoor gardens, terraces, and an indoor conservatory with exotic flora from all over the world.

Van Cortlandt Park — Van Cortlandt Park, located in hilly northwest Bronx, features great cycling and walking paths, beautiful oak forests, a public golf course, areas for relaxation and recreation, and a freshwater lake. The Old Croton Aqueduct Trail runs north-south through the park on top of the aqueduct that provided fresh water to New York City during the mid-1800s.

VISITOR INFORMATION

NYC Go
(800) NYC-VISIT
nycgo.com

Visit Westchester
(914) 995-8500
visitwestchesterny.com

Orchids at the New York Botanical Garden

The Met Cloisters

MAP 5   ARDSLEY - PLEASANTVILLE

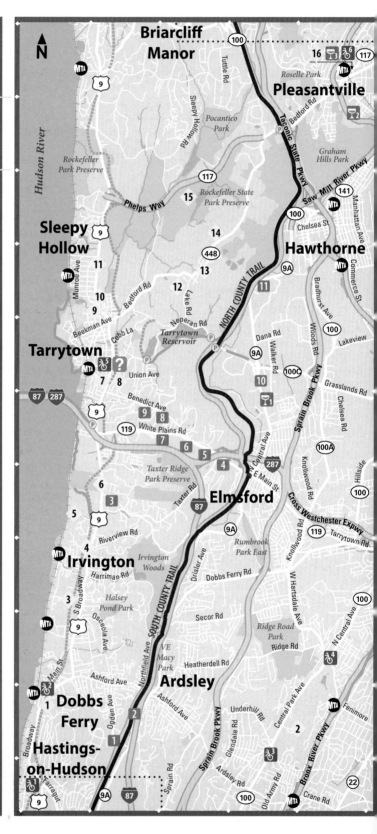

THINGS TO SEE & DO

#			
1.	Old Croton Aqueduct Keeper's House	15 Walnut St.	(914) 693-4117
2.	Greenburgh Nature Center	99 Dromore Rd.	(914) 723-3470
3.	The Armour-Stiner Octagon House	45 W Clinton Ave.	(914) 817-5763
4.	Irvington Historical Society	131 Main St.	(914) 591-1020
5.	Washington Irving's Sunnyside	3 W Sunnyside Ln.	(914) 366-6900
6.	Lyndhurst Mansion & Estate	635 S Broadway	(914) 631-4481
7.	Tarrytown Music Hall	13 Main St.	(914) 631-3390
8.	Historical Society Museum of Sleepy Hollow & Tarrytown	1 Grove St.	(914) 631-8374
9.	Philipsburg Manor	381 N Broadway	(914) 366-6900
10.	Old Dutch Reformed Church and Burying Grounds	430 N Broadway	(914) 631-4497
11.	Sleepy Hollow Cemetery	540 N Broadway	(914) 631-0081
12.	Kykuit, The Rockefeller Estate	200 Lake Rd.	(914) 366-6900
13.	Union Church of Pocantico Hills	555 Bedford Rd.	(914) 631-8923
14.	Stone Barns Center for Food & Agriculture	630 Bedford Rd.	(914) 366-6200
15.	Rockefeller State Park Preserve	125 Phelps Way	(914) 631-1470
16.	Jacob Burns Film Center	364 Manville Rd.	(914) 773-7663

TRAIL & TRAVEL NOTES

Historic Mansions — The post-Civil War industrial period created vast wealth for New York's so-called "robber barons," several of whom built large estates outside of New York City in Westchester County. Many are open to the public as historic sites, featuring Gilded Age architecture, impressive art collections, and beautiful antiques.

Haunted History — Washington Irving—who penned famous tales of Hudson Valley legends, including "Rip Van Winkle" and "The Legend of Sleepy Hollow"— lived in Irvington during the nineteenth century, and the village was later renamed in his honor. Irving's gothic stories blend local lore, real people and places, and fantasy fiction, and inspired the popular notion that the area is haunted.

VISITOR INFORMATION

Visit Westchester
(914) 995-8500
visitwestchesterny.com

Sleepy Hollow Tarrytown Chamber of Commerce
1 Neperan Rd.
(914) 631-1705
sleepyhollowtarrytownchamber.com

AMENITIES

| Elmsford | |
| Sleepy Hollow/Tarrytown | |

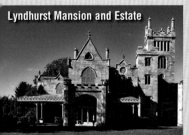
Lyndhurst Mansion and Estate

Illustration of Washington Irving's Sunnyside

MAP 6   BRIARCLIFF MANOR - YORKTOWN HEIGHTS

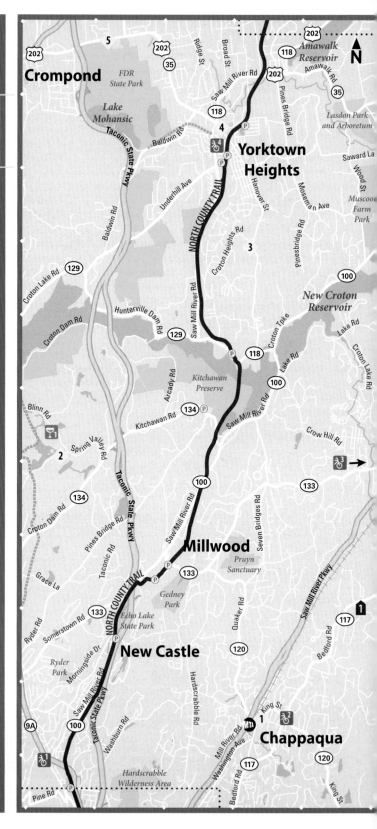

THINGS TO SEE & DO

1.	Horace Greeley House Museum	100 King St.	(914) 238-4666
2.	Teatown Lake Reservation	1600 Spring Valley Rd.	(914) 762-2912
3.	Hilltop Hanover Farm	1271 Hanover St.	(914) 862-5050
4.	Town of Yorktown Museum	1974 Commerce St.	(914) 962-2970
5.	Franklin D. Roosevelt State Park	2957 Crompond Rd.	(914) 245-4434

TRAIL & TRAVEL NOTES

Kitchawan Preserve — The North County Trailway runs through Kitchawan Preserve, which until 1989 was a research station for the Brooklyn Botanic Garden. Located along the New Croton Reservoir, the preserve's trails feature abundant migrating birds, butterflies, and native plants.

Yorktown History — Archeologists have dated the presence of Native people in Westchester County to at least 7,000 years ago. European settlement in Yorktown began in 1683. In 1781, Yorktown played a key role in the American Revolutionary War, as the only fixed crossing of the Croton River, the "Pines Bridge," was located there. The 1st Rhode Island Regiment, an integrated troop of Black, Indigenous, and colonial soldiers, guarded the bridge.

Thomas J. Watson Research Center — Since 1961, IBM Research headquarters, named after IBM founder Thomas J. Watson, have been located in Yorktown. Renowned architect Eero Saarinen designed the laboratory building, which houses several of the fastest supercomputers in the world. Notable company inventions include the floppy disk, the smartphone, the portable computer, the ATM, and the Watson artificial intelligence system.

VISITOR INFORMATION

Visit Westchester
(914) 995-8500
visitwestcherny.com

AMENITIES

Yorktown Heights

Riders on the trail in Yorktown Heights

Croton Reservoir

MAP 7

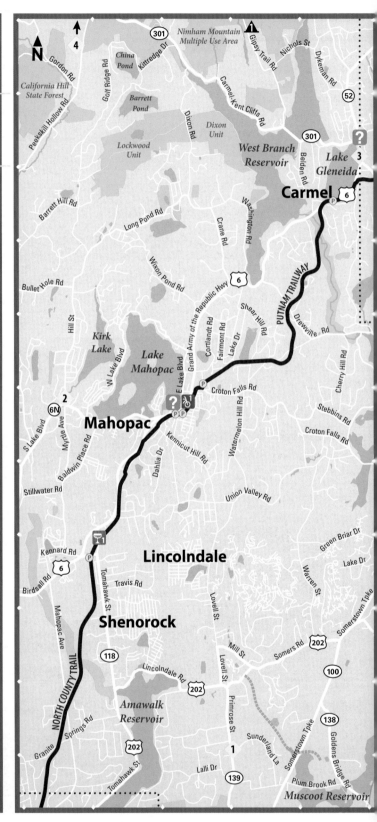

THINGS TO SEE & DO

1.	Wright Reis Homestead	94 Primrose St.	(914) 277-4977
2.	Red Mills Historic Park	23 Hill St.	
3.	Sybil Ludington Statue	15 Gleneida Ave.	
4.	Clarence Fahnestock State Park	1498 NYS Rte. 301	(845) 225-7207

TRAIL & TRAVEL NOTES

Lake Views — The Putnam Trailway, an off-road paved rail trail, travels past Lake Mahopac and Lake Gleneida, offering sparkling water views to trail users. One of Lake Mahopac's two islands is completely private, and features a Frank Lloyd Wright-inspired retrofuturistic home jutting out into the water.

The Philipse Patent — Adolphus Philipse, the son of a wealthy merchant family, purchased what is now Putnam County from Dutch traders in 1697, and the area was called The Philipse Patent for almost half a century afterwards. In 1766, tenants living in the Philipse Patent and other farmers marched on New York City to protest their rent payments. During the American Revolutionary War, rebels seized the land from the Philipse family because of their allegiance to the British. The Philipse family home in Yonkers is now a state historic site.

VISITOR INFORMATION

Mahopac-Carmel Chamber of Commerce
692 US Rte. 6
(845) 628-5553
mahopaccarmelonline.com

Putnam County Tourism
40 Gleneida Ave.
(845) 808-1015
putnamcountyny.com/tourputnam

AMENITIES

Mahopac	🍴🛒👜	Rx
Carmel Hamlet	🍴🛒👜👕	Rx

1975 stamp depicting Sybil Ludington's ride to rally Patriot soldiers during the Revolutionary War

Lake Mahopac

MAP 8   BREWSTER

THINGS TO SEE & DO

1.	Fred Dill Wildlife Sanctuary	62 Fair St.	(845) 808-1994
2.	Tilly Foster Farm Museum	100 NYS Rte. 312	(845) 808-1000
3.	Southeast Museum	67 Main St.	(845) 279-7500
4.	Wonder Lake State Park	380 Ludingtonville Rd.	(845) 225-7207
5.	Patterson Historical Society	1144 NYS Rte. 311	(845) 319-3071
6.	Gotham Woods	263 Holmes Rd.	(929) 324-1006
7.	Daryl's House Club	130 NYS Rte. 22	(845) 289-0185

TRAIL & TRAVEL NOTES

Brewster's Station — The town of Brewster, formerly known as "Brewster's Station," is named for Walter Brewster, who donated land to the New York and Harlem Railroad for a depot in 1848. Walter Brewster's original home is close to the Southeast Museum, which features exhibits on the history of the railroad.

The Oblong — The trail passes through the town of Patterson in the northeast corner of Putnam County. Patterson was originally settled in the eighteenth century in a region called The Oblong, the ownership of which was disputed between the New York and Connecticut colonies. Sybil Ludington, an American Revolutionary War hero who, when she was just 16, made a night-time ride to rally Patriot soldiers, was a famous resident of Patterson. She is memorialized in the town of Carmel with a prominent statue.

VISITOR INFORMATION

Putnam County Tourism
(845) 808-1015
putnamcountyny.com/tourputnam

Dutchess Tourism
(800) 445-3131
dutchesstourism.com

AMENITIES

Brewster

Tilly Foster Farm

Maybrook Trail

MAP 9   **HOPEWELL JUNCTION**   40

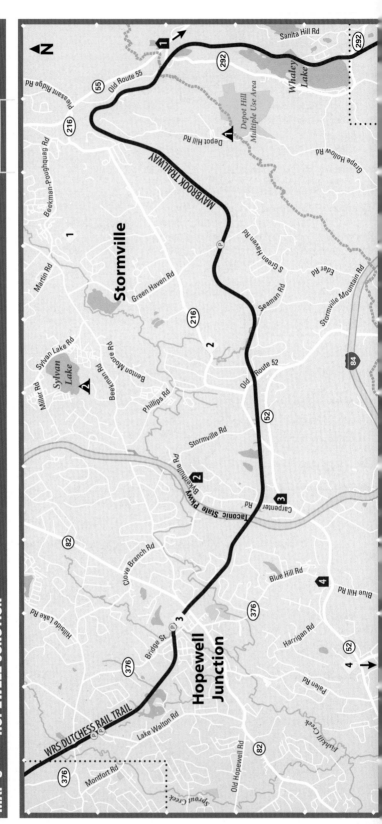

1 MILE

THINGS TO SEE & DO

1. Barton Orchards — 63 Apple Tree Ln. — (845) 227-2306
2. Stormville Airport Flea Market — 428 NYS Rte. 216 — (845) 221-6561
3. Hopewell Depot Museum — 36 Railroad Ave. — (845) 226-7003
4. The Barns Art Center — 736 South Dr.

TRAIL & TRAVEL NOTES

Appalachian Trail — The Appalachian Trail, a National Scenic Trail, stretches 2,200 miles from Springer Mountain in Georgia to Maine's Mount Katahdin. The Maybrook Trailway intersects the Appalachian Trail near the Depot Hill Multiple Use Area in West Pawling.

Hopewell Depot Museum — The hamlet of Hopewell Junction formed in 1869 around the confluence of three railroad lines - the Dutchess and Columbia Railroad, the Boston, Hartford and Erie Railroad, and the Dutchess County Railroad, which became known as the Maybrook Line. These original railroads changed hands and names several times, as nineteenth century railroad networks grew rapidly to accommodate trade between city centers and rural areas. The Hopewell Depot Museum, located in a replica restoration of the original 1873 station, features exhibits on railroad history and the local area.

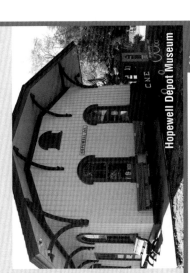

Hopewell Depot Museum

VISITOR INFORMATION

Dutchess Tourism
(800) 445-3131
dutchesstourism.com

AMENITIES

Hopewell Junction ⊕ 🛏 🍴 🏕 🛍 👫 Rx

Dutchess County is home to many apple orchards

41

MAP 10 POUGHKEEPSIE

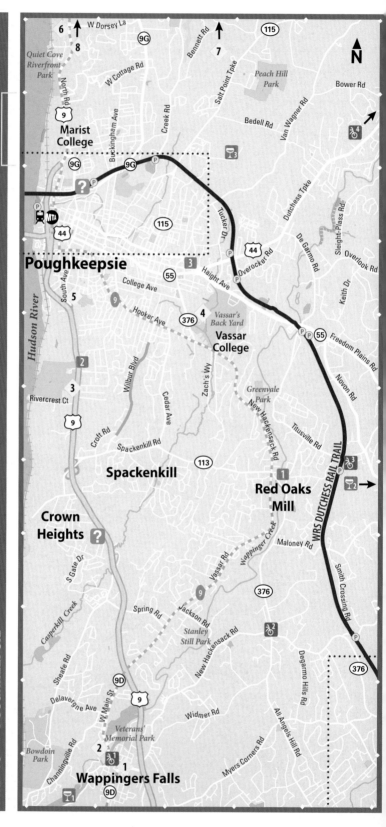

THINGS TO SEE & DO

1.	Mesier Homestead and Museum	2 Spring St.	(845) 632-1281
2.	County Players Falls Theater	2681 W Main St.	(845) 298-1491
3.	Locust Grove Estate	2683 South Rd.	(845) 454-4500
4.	Vassar College	124 Raymond Ave.	(845) 437-7000
	Frances Lehman Loeb Art Center	124 Raymond Ave.	(845) 437-5237
5.	Springside National Historic Site	185 Academy St.	(845) 454-2060
6.	The Culinary Institute of America	1946 Campus Dr.	(845) 452-9600
7.	Eleanor Roosevelt National Historic Site	56 Valkill Park Rd.	(845) 229-9422
8.	Home of Franklin D. Roosevelt National Historic Site	4097 Albany Post Rd.	(845) 229-5320

TRAIL & TRAVEL NOTES

Wappinger Culture — The Mesier Homestead and Museum holds an extensive collection of artifacts from the Wappinger people, who inhabited a territory stretching from Albany to New York City prior to European settlement. The collection includes arrowheads, spear points, and tools, dating as far back as 8,500 years ago.

"There are many ways of going forward, but only one way of standing still."
President Franklin D. Roosevelt was born in Hyde Park at Springwood House, now a historic site open to the public. The site, with extensive gardens and trails showcasing views of the Hudson Valley and Hudson River, offers tours of the home and the first presidential library. Eleanor Roosevelt's residence, Val-Kill, located adjacent to Springwood and also open for tours, is the nation's only historic site dedicated to a First Lady.

VISITOR INFORMATION

Dutchess Tourism
3 Neptune Rd.
(800) 445-3131
dutchesstourism.com

AMENITIES

Wappingers Falls

Franklin and Eleanor Roosevelt, 1905

Autumn in Poughkeepsie

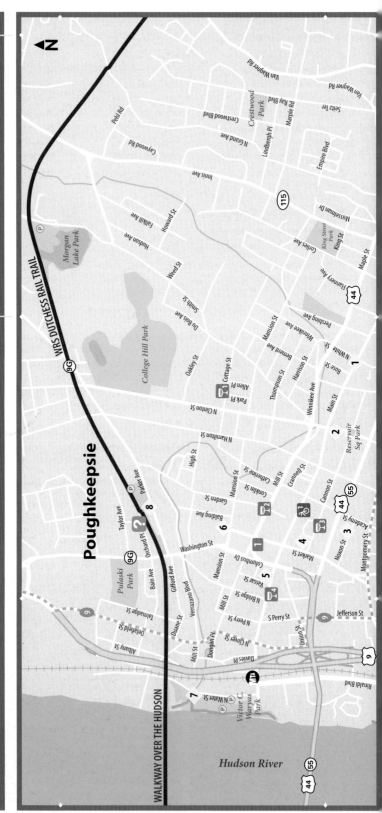

1 MILE

N

Poughkeepsie

WALKWAY OVER THE HUDSON

WRS DUTCHESS RAIL TRAIL

Hudson River

College Hill Park

Morgan Lake Park

Pulaski Park

Victor C. Waryas Park

Crestwood Park

King Street Park

Reservoir Sq Park

THINGS TO SEE & DO

1. Clinton House State Historic Site — 549 Main St. — (845) 471-1630
2. Womenswork.Art/Clinton Street Studio — 4 S Clinton St.
3. Barrett Art Center — 55 Noxon St. — (845) 471-2550
4. Bardavon 1869 Opera House — 35 Market St. — (845) 473-2072
5. Cunneen-Hackett Arts Center — 9 Vassar St. — (845) 486-4571
6. Poughkeepsie Post Office — 55 Mansion St. — (845) 452-5297
7. Mid-Hudson Children's Museum — 75 N Water St. — (845) 471-0589
8. Walkway Over the Hudson State Historic Park — 61 Parker Ave. — (845) 454-9649

TRAIL & TRAVEL NOTES

Historic State Capital — Named for George Clinton, the first Governor of New York, the Clinton House State Historic Site was an important meeting place for state legislators between 1777 and 1783 when Poughkeepsie served as the State Capital. Today the site houses archives and a library for local historical research.

Heart of Downtown — Dubbed the "Queen City of the Hudson" during the Gilded Age, Poughkeepsie has undergone a renaissance in recent years. Easy access to New York City by train, historic architecture and gorgeous views of the Hudson River have combined to give rise to a vibrant arts and entertainment scene.

Walkway Over the Hudson State Historic Park — The iconic Walkway opened in 2009, as the world's longest elevated pedestrian and bicycling bridge, offering 360 degree views of the Hudson River. The Walkway sits atop a 212-foot-high railroad bridge constructed in 1889 and partially destroyed by a fire in 1974.

VISITOR INFORMATION

Dutchess Tourism
(800) 445-3131
dutchesstourism.com

Walkway Over the Hudson Welcome Centers
27 Orchard Place
(845) 454-9649
walkway.org

AMENITIES

Poughkeepsie 🍴 🛒 ⛽ 🚻 Rx

A family enjoying the Walkway

45

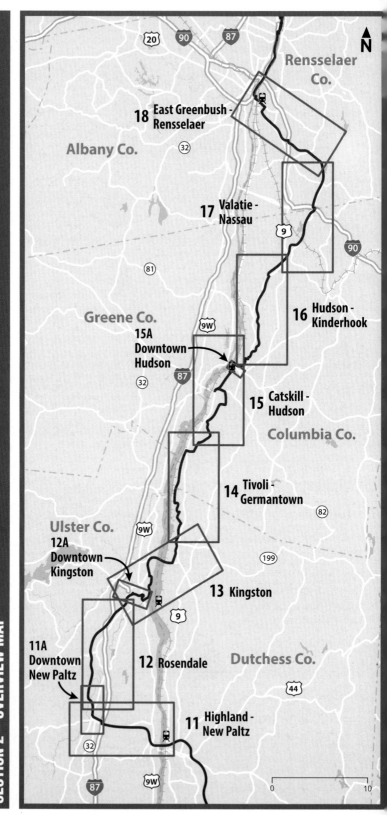

N

20 I-90 87

Rensselaer Co.

18 East Greenbush - Rensselaer

Albany Co. 32

17 Valatie - Nassau 9 I-90

81

Greene Co. 9W

15A Downtown Hudson

16 Hudson - Kinderhook

32 I-87

15 Catskill - Hudson

Columbia Co.

14 Tivoli - Germantown 82

Ulster Co. 9W

12A Downtown Kingston

199

13 Kingston

9

11A Downtown New Paltz

12 Rosendale

Dutchess Co.

44

11 Highland - New Paltz

32

I-87 9W

0   10

SECTION 2

POUGHKEEPSIE TO ALBANY

The northern half of the Hudson River Valley Greenway Trail connects Poughkeepsie to Albany. This 99-mile leg consists of Walkway Over the Hudson State Historic Park, the Hudson Valley Rail Trail, the Wallkill Valley Rail Trail, on-road sections, and the Albany-Hudson Electric Trail.

Walkway Over the Hudson State Historic Park soars dramatically over the Hudson River, connecting Poughkeepsie with Highland on the western shore. The Hudson River Valley Greenway Trail travels west from the Highland end of the Walkway along the Hudson Valley Rail Trail. This paved, 9-mile off-road trail runs to New Paltz. A 2-mile route through New Paltz is currently on-road.

From New Paltz to Kingston, the trail follows the northernmost 13 miles of the Wallkill Valley Rail Trail, which has a stone dust surface. The 6.5-mile route through Kingston features two short, yet inviting, off-road trail segments (the Kingston Point Rail Trail and the Hudson River Brickyard Trail in Sojourner Truth State Park), connected by a mix of on-road routes. Some of the on-road sections have painted bike lanes, while others only rely on shared lane markings and signage to delineate the route.

The north end of the Hudson River Brickyard Trail marks the beginning of a 35-mile on-road route between the cities of Kingston and Hudson. A few sections are on the shoulders of busy state highways, but most of the route follows scenic, lower-traffic rural roads. The trail route returns to the east side of the Hudson by crossing the 1.5-mile Kingston-Rhinecliff Bridge. Bicyclists can ride on the road's shoulders or dismount and walk on the protected sidewalk. Once on the eastern side, the route passes north through the Bard College campus. The route is well-marked with Empire State Trail signage, but be mindful of student pedestrian traffic. North of Bard College, the route includes a 1.5-mile off-road trail through the Tivoli Bays Wildlife Management Area. From Tivoli to Hudson, the route is on-road, and is only appropriate for experienced bicyclists comfortable riding next to vehicle traffic. In Hudson, the trail primarily runs along city streets.

In the town of Greenport, 2 miles north of Hudson, the off-road Albany-Hudson Electric Trail begins its 32-mile run north. The majority of this trail is off-road, with paved and stone dust surfaces, interspersed with a few brief on-road sections. The northern end of the trail is in East Greenbush, and 3 miles of on-road riding on fairly busy roads connect the trail through the city of Rensselaer. This on-road route follows a steep descent to the water level of the Hudson River. Use caution on city streets where it is easy to pick up speed on the descent and traffic can be heavy at times.

The trail crosses the Hudson River on a protected sidewalk of the Dunn Memorial Bridge. The entrance to the sidewalk is on Broadway just south of 4th Avenue.

COMMUNITIES ALONG ROUTE

Ulster County	Highland, New Paltz, Rosendale, Kingston, Ulster
Dutchess County	Rhinebeck, Red Hook, Annandale-on-Hudson, Tivoli
Columbia County	Germantown, Greenport, Hudson, Kinderhook, Valatie, Chatham
Rensselaer County	Nassau, East Greenbush, Rensselaer

VISITOR INFORMATION

Ulster County	ulstercountyalive.com	(800) 342-5826
Dutchess County	dutchesstourism.com	(845) 463-4000
Columbia County	columbiacountytourism.org	(518) 828-3375
Rensselaer County	renscotourism.com	(518) 270-2673

SAFETY & SECURITY

Universal Emergency Number: 911

Law Enforcement

State Police Troop F	Ulster County	(845) 344-5300
State Police Troop K	Dutchess and Columbia Counties	(845) 677-7300
State Police Troop G	Rensselaer and Albany Counties	(518) 783-3211
Ulster County Sheriff	Kingston	(845) 338-3640
Dutchess County Sheriff	Poughkeepsie	(845) 486-3800
Columbia County Sheriff	Hudson	(518) 828-0601
Rensselaer County Sheriff	Troy	(518) 266-1900
Albany County Sheriff	Albany	(518) 487-5400

Cyclists on the Rosendale Trestle

TRANSPORTATION

Amtrak Rail Stations (800-USA-RAIL)   amtrak.com
Poughkeepsie (Amtrak and Metro-North)   41 Main St.
Rhinecliff   455 Rhinecliff Rd.
Hudson   69 S Front St.
Rensselaer   525 East St.

Major Bus Stations
Trailways Bus Terminal - Kingston   400 Washington Ave.   (800) 858-8555
Trailways Bus Terminal - New Paltz   139 Main St.   (800) 858-8555
OurBus/Megabus - Rensselaer   525 East St.   megabus.us
Albany Bus Terminal   34 Hamilton St.   (518) 427-7060

Urban & Regional Transit
Ulster County Area Transit   ucat.ulstercountyny.gov   (888) 827-8228
Dutchess County Public Transit   dutchessny.gov   (845) 473-8424
Capital District Transportation Authority cdta.org   (518) 482-8822

Commercial Airports
Albany International Airport   albanyairport.com   (518) 242-2222

HOSPITALS

Northern Dutchess Hospital   Rhinebeck   (845) 876-3001
Columbia Memorial Hospital   Hudson   (518) 828-7601
HealthAlliance Hospital Mary's Avenue Campus   Kingston   (845) 331-3131
HealthAlliance Hospital Broadway Campus   Kingston   (845) 331-3131
Albany Medical Center Hospital   Albany   (518) 262-3125
Albany Memorial Hospital   Albany   (518) 471-3221
St. Peter's Hospital   Albany   (518) 525-1550

Waterfall views along the Albany Hudson Electric Trail

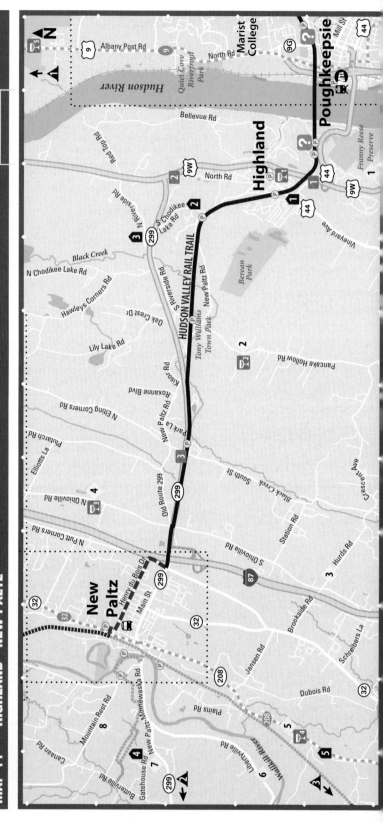

THINGS TO SEE & DO

1. Franny Reese State Park — 129 Macks Ln. — (845) 473-4440
2. Wilklow Orchards — 341 Pancake Hollow Rd. — (845) 691-2339
3. Minard's Family Farm — 250 Hurds Rd. — (845) 325-0222
4. Twin Star Orchards — 155 N Ohioville Rd. — (845) 633-8657
5. Dressel Farms — 271 NYS Rte. 208 — (845) 255-0693
6. Ulster County Fairgrounds — 249 Libertyville Rd. — (845) 255-1380
7. Mohonk Preserve — 35 NYS Rte. 299 — (845) 255-0919
8. Unison Arts and Learning Center — 68 Mountain Rest Rd. — (845) 255-1559

Riders on the Hudson Valley Rail Trail

TRAIL & TRAVEL NOTES

Hudson Valley Apple Trail — Connecting seven family-owned and operated apple orchards along a loop in Ulster County, the 25-mile Hudson Valley Apple Trail provides opportunities to visit the farms to pick up the region's iconic apples, cider, and donuts. An upsurge of interest in the humble fruit over the past decade has boosted the number of apple varieties, ciders, liqueurs, and sundry products available. New York is the second-largest apple producer in the United States, and the Hudson Valley produces 20 percent of New York apples.

The Shawangunks — Locally known as "the Gunks," this mountain range looms high over New Paltz. The Shawangunk Ridge, part of the Appalachians, runs from northern New Jersey to the Catskills. The Gunks are a major destination for rock-climbers, hikers, mountain bikers, and other outdoor enthusiasts. The Mohonk Preserve, which spans 8,000 acres of forests, fields, cliffs, caves, and streams, provides access to the ridge. Nearby Minnewaska State Park Preserve covers a wide expanse of the ridge as well, with 33 miles of carriage roads and 50 miles of footpaths.

Mohonk Preserve Testimonial Gateway

VISITOR INFORMATION

Ulster County Alive
(800) 342-5826
ulstercountyalive.com

AMENITIES

Highland

🛈 🍴 🛍 🎁 ℞

51

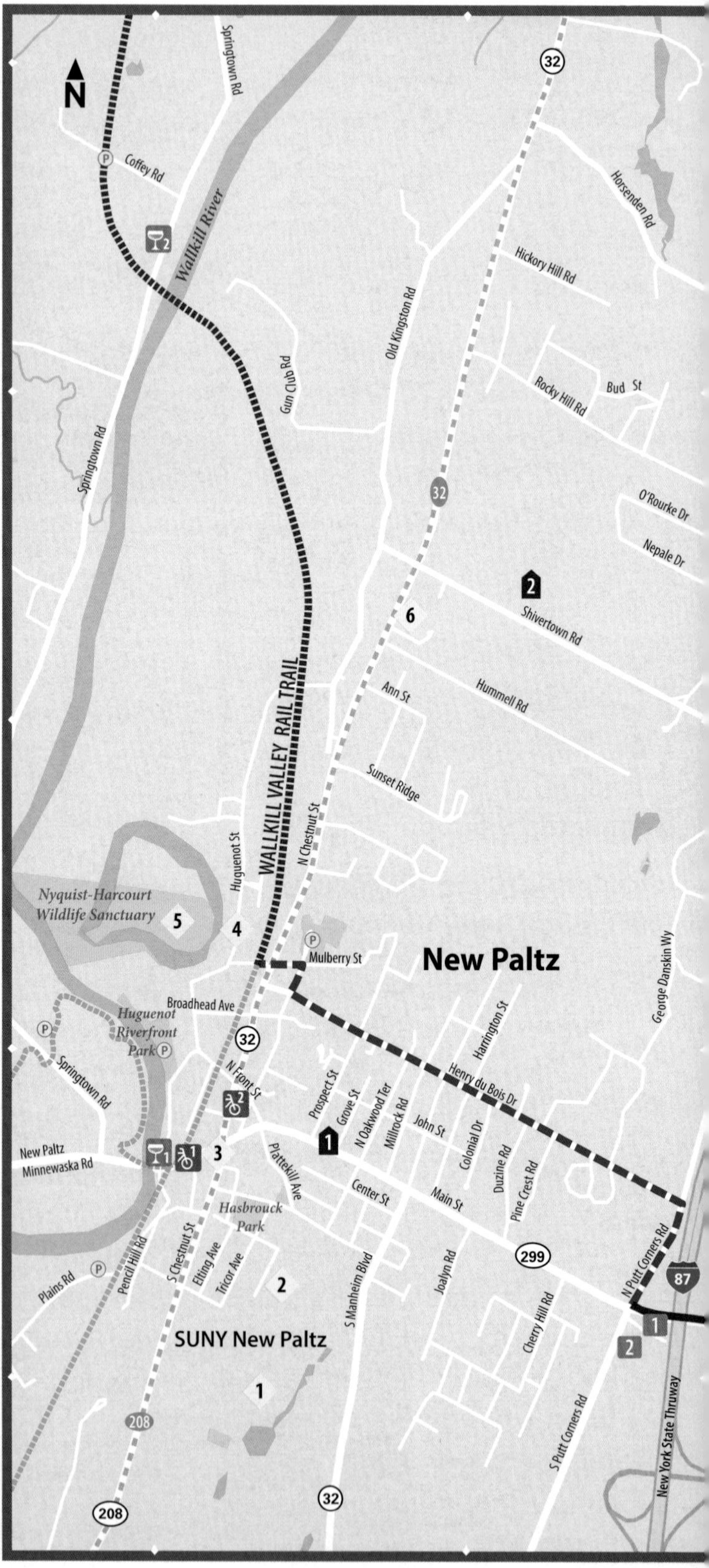

N

Springtown Rd

Coffey Rd

Wallkill River

32

Horsenden Rd

Hickory Hill Rd

Gun Club Rd

Old Kingston Rd

Rocky Hill Rd

Bud St

Springtown Rd

32

O'Rourke Dr

Nepale Dr

2

Shivertown Rd

WALLKILL VALLEY RAIL TRAIL

6

Ann St

Hummell Rd

Huguenot St

N Chestnut St

Sunset Ridge

Nyquist-Harcourt
Wildlife Sanctuary

5

4

New Paltz

George Danskin Wy

Mulberry St

Broadhead Ave

Huguenot
Riverfront
Park

P

Springtown Rd

32

N Front St

Prospect St

Grove St

N Oakwood Ter

Millock Rd

John St

Henry du Bois Dr

Harrington St

Colonial Dr

Duzine Rd

Pine Crest Rd

New Paltz
Minnewaska Rd

3

1

Center St

Main St

Plattekill Ave

Pencil Hill Rd

Plains Rd

S Chestnut St

Elting Ave

Tricor Ave

Hasbrouck
Park

2

S Manheim Blvd

Joalyn Rd

299

Cherry Hill Rd

N Putt Corners Rd

87

1

2

SUNY New Paltz

1

New York State Thruway

208

32

S Putt Corners Rd

208

THINGS TO SEE & DO

1.	SUNY New Paltz	1 Hawk Dr.	(845) 257-7869
	Samuel Dorsky Museum of Art	Smiley Art Bldg.	(845) 257-3844
	Smolen Observatory	Smolen Observatory	(845) 257-1110
2.	John R. Kirk Planetarium	Coykendall Science Bldg.	(845) 257-3818
3.	Alpine Endeavors	44 Main St.	(877) 486-5769
4.	Historic Huguenot Street	Huguenot St.	(845) 255-1660
5.	Nyquist-Harcourt Wildlife Sanctuary	133 Huguenot St.	(845) 255-3003
6.	Apple Hill Farm	124 NYS Rte. 32 S	(845) 255-1605

TRAIL & TRAVEL NOTES

Huguenot Street — Huguenot Street's seven stone houses date back to the early 18th century, providing a glimpse into the lives of New Paltz's French Protestant settlers. Huguenots first began to colonize New Paltz in 1678, moving onto land then occupied by the Esopus, a tribe of the Lenape people. Now a National Historic Landmark Site and a Maurice D. Hinchey Hudson River Valley National Heritage Area Site, Historic Huguenot Street offers guided tours, special events, and a collection of archives and artifacts pertaining to Indigenous peoples, African American history, the colonial experience, and the Civil War. The Historic Huguenot Street Walking Tour app offers the option for independent tours, including a Haunted Tour option for the paranormally-inclined.

College Town — New Paltz has been an educational center for almost 200 years; the State University of New York at New Paltz can trace its history back to the New Paltz Classical School, a secondary school founded in 1828. Downtown New Paltz reflects the energy and creativity of the student population, with many unique and eccentric stores, art galleries, bars, and restaurants lining Main Street.

VISITOR INFORMATION

Ulster County Alive
(800) 342-5826
ulstercountyalive.com

AMENITIES

New Paltz

Morning mist around the Shawangunk Ridge

Water Street Market, New Paltz

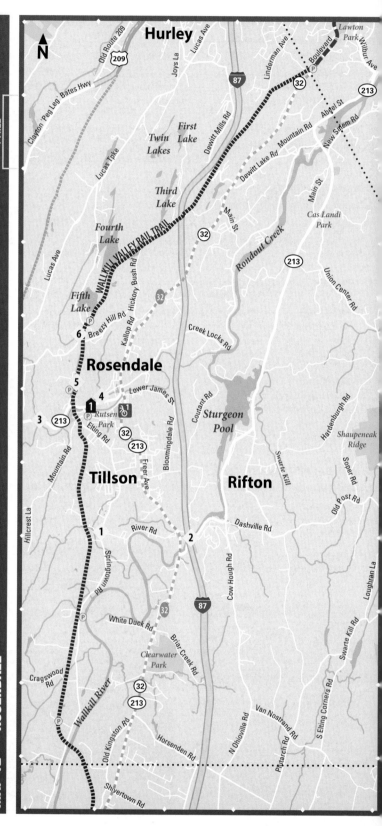

MAP 12 ROSENDALE

THINGS TO SEE & DO

1.	Stone Mountain Farm	310 River Rd. Ext.	
2.	Perrine's Covered Bridge	NYS Rte. 213	
3.	The Snyder Estate & Widow Jane Mine	668 NYS Rte. 213	(845) 658-9900
4.	Rosendale Theatre	408 Main St.	(845) 658-8989
5.	Rosendale Trestle	Mountain Rd.	(845) 255-2761
6.	Women's Studio Workshop	722 Binnewater Ln.	(845) 658-9133

TRAIL & TRAVEL NOTES

Wallkill Valley Rail Trail — The Wallkill Valley Rail Trail, which was resurfaced with new stonedust in 2021, follows the route of the former Wallkill Valley Railroad, which hosted trains between 1866 and 1977. Spanning 22 miles from Gardiner to Kingston, the multi-use trail welcomes pedestrians, runners, cyclists, and equestrians and features beautiful views of the Catskill Mountains and the sparkling waters of the Wallkill River and Rondout Creek, as well as the intriguing remains of past industrial structures. Some of the visible ruins are related to the production of Rosendale cement, a natural hydraulic cement used in the construction of the Statue of Liberty, Federal Hall, the Brooklyn Bridge, and the U.S. Capitol building.

Water Under the Bridge — A centerpiece of the Wallkill Valley Rail Trail is the beautifully restored Rosendale Trestle, a former truss railroad bridge that soars over the Rondout Creek. Rising 150 feet, it had the highest span of any bridge in the United States when it opened in 1872. The Trestle's spectacular views are not to be missed.

VISITOR INFORMATION

Ulster County Alive
(800) 342-5826
ulstercountyalive.com

AMENITIES

Rosendale

Old D&H Canal Postcard, Rosendale, 1912

Rosendale Trestle along the Wallkill Valley Rail Trail

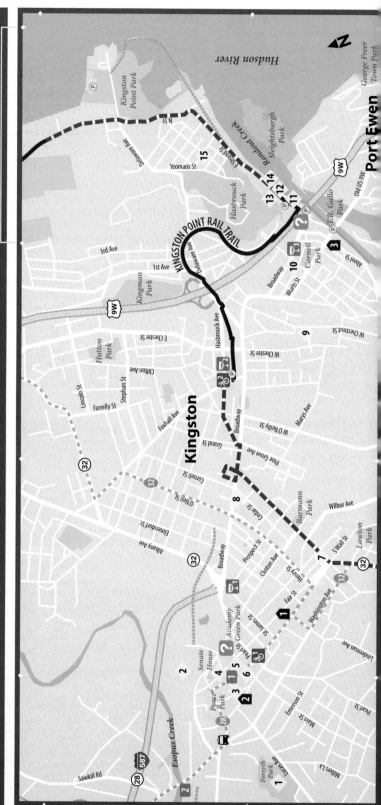

1 MILE

N

Hudson River

Kingston Point Park

P

Delaware Ave

Kingston Point Rail Trail

1st St N

Esopus Creek

Rondout Creek

Sleightsburgh Park

George Freer Town Park

Port Ewen

9W

Old US 9W

T.R. Gallo Park

P

P

P ? 11 12 13 14

15

Yeomans St

Hasbrouck Park

E Strand

Hasbrouck Ave

3rd Ave

1st Ave

Delaware Ave

P ? 3

Abeel St

3

Cornell Park

10 ? 3

Broadway

Wurts St

9W

Kingman Park

Hutton Park

E Chester St

Clifton Ave

Stephan St

Farrelly St

Lincoln St

32

W Chester St

9

W Chestnut St

Mary's Ave

? 2

P

Kingston

Broadway

Grand St

Cornell St

O'Neil St

Foxhall Ave

W O'Reilly St

Pine Grove Ave

Barmann Park

Wilbur Ave

Lawton Park

S Wall St

32

Elmendorf St

Albany Ave

32

Broadway

Cedar St

8

Prospect St

Clinton Ave

Henry St

Washington Ave

Lindeman Ave

7

32

1

Fair St

? 1

Academy Green Park

St James St

Pearl St

Emerson St

Main St

Pearl St

Senate House

? 4 1 5

2 3 2 6 ?

28

Peace Park

2

587

28

Sawkill Rd

Esopus Creek

Forsyth Park

Lucas Ave

Millers La

THINGS TO SEE & DO

1.	Forsyth Nature Center	125 Lucas Ave. Ext.	(845) 339-3053
2.	Catskill Mountain Railroad	55 Plaza Rd.	(845) 332-4854
3.	Matthewis Persen House Museum	74 John St.	(845) 340-3040
4.	Senate House State Historic Site	296 Fair St.	(845) 338-2786
5.	Old Dutch Church	272 Wall St.	(845) 338-6759
6.	Fred J. Johnston House Museum & Gallery	63 Main St.	(845) 339-0720
7.	Green Kill	229 Greenkill Rd.	(347) 689-2323
8.	Ulster Performing Arts Center	601 Broadway	(845) 339-6088
9.	Coach House Theatre	12 Augusta St.	(845) 331-2476
10.	Reher Center for Immigrant Culture and History	99-101 Broadway	(845) 481-3738
11	Hudson River Maritime Museum	50 Rondout Landing	(845) 338-0071
12.	Tivoli Sailing Company	100 E Strand St.	(845) 901-2697
13.	Trolley Museum of New York	89 E Strand St.	(845) 331-3399
14.	ArtPort Kingston	108 E Strand St.	
15.	A.J. Williams-Myers African Roots Center	43 Gill St.	(845) 802-0035

Kingston waterfront

TRAIL & TRAVEL NOTES

"If it is not a fit place for women, it is unfit for men to be there." — Sojourner Truth, abolitionist and women's rights activist, was born into slavery just outside of Kingston. Truth escaped to gain freedom in her late twenties, and spent the rest of her life fighting for civil rights. Her extraordinary bravery and life's work is commemorated in statues across the country, including in the U.S. Capitol building and on the west side of the Walkway Over the Hudson.

Maritime Village — The Rondout, a popular Kingston destination along the Hudson River at the mouth of Rondout Creek, was a separate village prior to 1872. The port was once the third largest along the Hudson, developed as a result of the completion of the Delaware and Hudson Canal. Today, the charming waterside Rondout neighborhood features museums, an active marina and many varied eateries, and hosts artistic and historic events.

Fun Festivities — Kingston is home to numerous festivals throughout the year, including the Artists Soapbox Derby, the O+ Festival, the Kingston Multicultural Festival, the MAD Celebration of the Arts, and the Ulster County Italian Festival.

VISITOR INFORMATION

Ulster County Alive
244 Fair St.
(800) 342-5826
ulstercountyalive.com

Kingston Heritage Area Visitors Center
20 Broadway
(800) 342-5826
ulstercountyalive.com

AMENITIES

Kingston

57

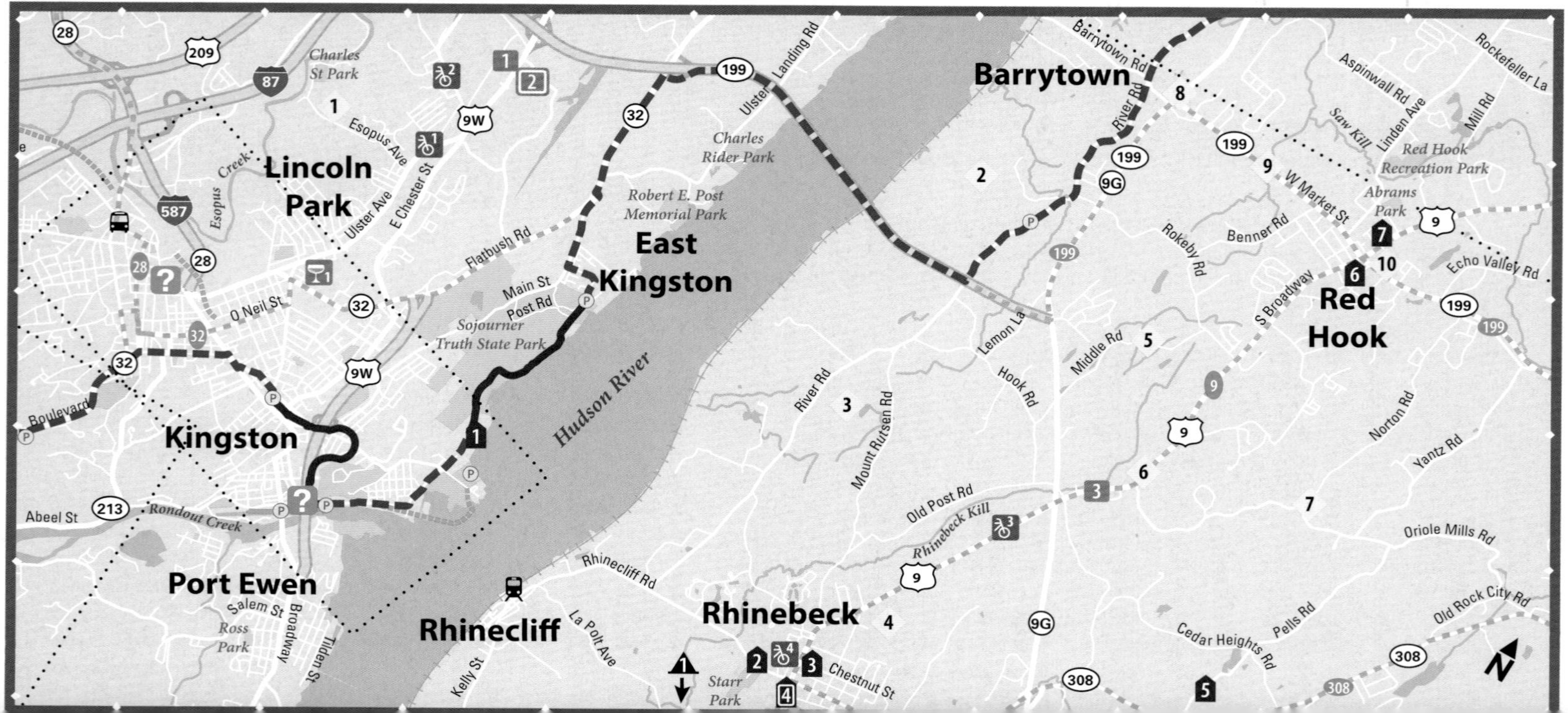

MAP 13   KINGSTON

1 MILE

N

Barrytown

Red Hook

Rhinebeck

Rhinecliff

East Kingston

Lincoln Park

Kingston

Port Ewen

Hudson River

Rockefeller La

Mill Rd

Aspinwall Ave

Linden Ave

Red Hook Recreation Park

Saw Kill

Abrams Park

Echo Valley Rd

199

9

7

10

6

W Market St

9

S Broadway

Bennar Rd

Rokeby Rd

Norton Rd

Yantz Rd

Oriole Mills Rd

Old Rock City Rd

308

Pells Rd

7

Cedar Heights Rd

5

199

8

River Rd

Barrytown Rd

199

9G

199

Lemon La

Hook Rd

Middle Rd

5

9

9

6

3

9G

308

2

Mount Rutsen Rd

River Rd

3

Olde Post Rd

Rhinebeck Kill

9

4

3

199

Ulster Landing Rd

32

Charles Rider Park

Robert E. Post Memorial Park

2

4

6

3

Chestnut St

4

Starr Park

Rhinecliff Rd

La Polt Ave

Kelly St

Main St

Post Rd

Flatbush Rd

Sojourner Truth State Park

1

Tilden St

Broadway

Salem St

Ross Park

Rondout Creek

Esopus Creek

Charles St Park

87

209

28

Esopus Ave

Ulster Ave

E Chester St

1

2

9W

1

28

28

587

32

9W

32

O'Neil St

1

?

?

?

32

Boulevard

Abeel St

213

28

THINGS TO SEE & DO

1.	Seed Song Farm & Center	160 Esopus Ave.	(845) 383-1528
2.	Poet's Walk Park	776 River Rd.	(845) 473-4440
3.	Ferncliff Forest	68 Mount Rutsen Rd.	(845) 876-1559
4.	Dutchess County Fairgrounds	6636 US Rte. 9	(845) 876-4000
5.	Kesicke Farm	229 Middle Rd.	(845) 590-9642
6.	Museum of Rhinebeck History	7015 US Rte. 9 N	(845) 554-6331
7.	Old Rhinebeck Aerodrome	9 Norton Rd.	(845) 752-3200
8.	Montgomery Place Orchards	4283 NYS Rte. 9G	(845) 758-5476
9.	Hardeman Orchards	193 W Market St.	(845) 656-8538
10.	Equis Art Gallery	15 W Market St.	(845) 758-9432
	Historic Red Hook at the Elmendorph Inn	7562 North Broadway	(845) 758-1920

Cyclists and walkers enjoy the view at Poet's Walk Park

TRAIL & TRAVEL NOTES

Romantic Landscapes — Poet's Walk Park in Red Hook, designed during the mid-nineteenth century when landscape architecture was gaining prominence, features natural tree and rock wall demarcations to create a sense of distinct outdoor spaces. From the park entrance, the trail leads to an open air pavilion with stunning views across the Hudson River to the Catskills. The park's name commemorates the many writers who loved to walk there, including Washington Irving who, in his autobiography, wrote, "of all the scenery of the Hudson, the Kaatskill Mountains had the most witching effect on my boyish imagination."

Flying High — The Old Rhinebeck Aerodrome, America's first museum of antique aircraft, contains small engine planes from the earliest prototypes of air travel to the "Golden Age" of flight between the World Wars. The Aerodrome offers seasonal air shows for spectators and biplane rides for those who want to experience the excitement firsthand.

An abundance of local produce

VISITOR INFORMATION

Ulster County Alive
244 Fair St.
(800) 342-5826
ulstercountyalive.com

Dutchess Tourism
(800) 445-3131
dutchesstourism.com

AMENITIES

Rhinebeck   ⊕ 🛏 🍴 👕   Rx

MAP 14 — TIVOLI - GERMANTOWN

THINGS TO SEE & DO

1.	Montgomery Place Historic Estate	26 Gardener Way	(845) 752-5000
2.	Hessel Museum of Art	33 Garden Rd.	(845) 758-7598
3.	Bard College	Campus Rd.	(845) 758-7472
4.	Richard B. Fisher Center for the Performing Arts	60 Manor Ave.	(845) 758-7900
5.	Rose Hill Farm	19 Rose Hill Farm Rd.	(845) 758-4215
6.	Greig Farm	227 Pitcher Ln.	(845) 758-8007
7.	Mead Orchards	15 Scism Rd.	(845) 756-5641
8.	Kaatsbaan Cultural Park	120 Broadway	(518) 757-5106
9.	Tivoli Artists Gallery	60 Broadway	(845) 757-2667
10.	Clermont State Historic Site	1 Clermont Ave.	(518) 537-4240
11.	Germantown History Department	52 Maple Ave.	(518) 537-3600
12.	Keep Conservation Foundation Preserve	525 County Rte. 8	
13.	Spring Wind Farm	71 Hill-N-Dale Rd.	(518) 537-5161

TRAIL & TRAVEL NOTES

A Rich Wetland Ecosystem — Tivoli Bays is one of four sites in the Hudson River National Estuarine Research Reserve, preserved for research, monitoring, and education. Estuaries are unique aquatic ecosystems in which freshwater rivers or streams meet saltwater to create a brackish environment. Visitors to Tivoli Bays can hike or kayak around the intertidal swamp, coves, marshes, hills, shoreline, bedrock islands, and tributary mouths, guided by informational kiosks. Tivoli Bays is recognized as an important habitat for many songbirds, marsh birds, and raptors, including bald eagles and ospreys.

Wine and Roses — Dutchess and Columbia Counties offer a bounty of fresh produce and fine wines, with many historic and family-owned farms. Rose Hill Farm, a pick-your-own fruit orchard in Red Hook, was first established in 1798.

VISITOR INFORMATION

Dutchess Tourism
(800) 445-3131
dutchesstourism.com

AMENITIES

Tivoli	🍴🛒
Germantown	🍴🛒👕👕
Red Hook	🍴🛒👕👕 ℞

Lush grounds at Clermont State Historic Site

Richard B. Fisher Center at Bard College

1 MILE

MAP 15 CATSKILL - HUDSON

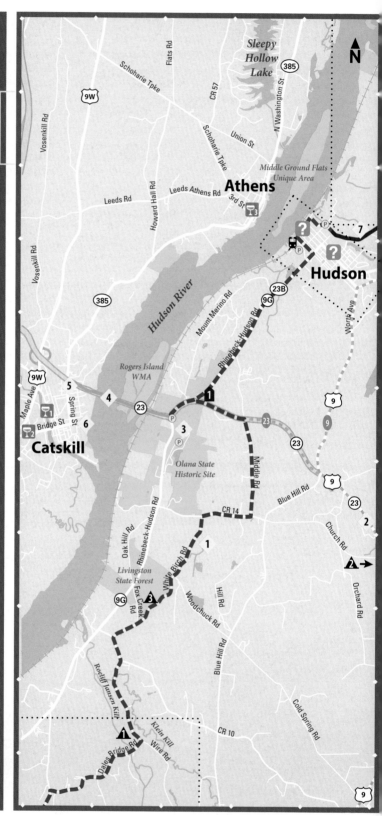

THINGS TO SEE & DO

1.	Fix Bros Fruit Farm	215 White Birch Rd.	(518) 828-4401
2.	Meisner's Heritage Farm	3771 US Rte. 9	(518) 965-9279
3.	Olana State Historic Site	5720 NYS Rte. 9G	(518) 828-1872
4.	Hudson River Skywalk	Rip Van Winkle Bridge	
5.	Thomas Cole National Historic Site	218 Spring St.	(518) 943-7465
6.	Beattie-Powers Place	10 Powers Pl.	
7.	FASNY Museum of Firefighting	117 Harry Howard Ave.	(518) 822-1875

TRAIL & TRAVEL NOTES

"Nature has been very lavish here in the gift of her beauty." — Olana, home to Hudson River School painter Frederic Edwin Church, sits atop 250 acres overlooking the Hudson River and is a must-see state historic site. Renowned architect and landscape designer Calvert Vaux, co-designer of Central Park in NYC, worked with Church to create an eclectic villa featuring a unique blend of Victorian, Moorish, and Persian architecture. The Hudson River School of painting is a nineteenth century movement in American art typified by dramatic, lush outdoor scenes. The founder of the movement and Church's teacher, Thomas Cole, lived and worked just across the river in Catskill.

Hudson River Skywalk — The Rip Van Winkle Bridge, named after the eponymous Washington Irving tale which takes place in the Catskills, offers panoramic views of the Hudson Valley between Hudson and Catskill. The bridge's walkway, re-imagined and re-designed with lookouts and interpretive signage, is now known as the Hudson River Skywalk. The pedestrian walkway connects two historic sites - Frederic Church's Olana and Thomas Cole's Cedar Grove. Cycling is not allowed on the Skywalk but cyclists may dismount and walk their bikes, or choose to cycle across the bridge on the roadway.

VISITOR INFORMATION

Columbia County Tourism
401 State St.
(518) 828-3375
columbiacountytourism.org

Columbia County Chamber of Commerce
1 North Front St.
(518) 828-4417
cityofhudson.org

AMENITIES

Catskill

Hudson River School of Art – *The Catskills*, Asher Brown Durand, 1859

Olana State Historic Site

1 MILE

N

Hudson River

Hudson

Promenade Hill Park

Henry Hudson Riverfront Park

7th Street Park

Washington Park

Fairview Ave

Prospect Ave

Worth Ave

Columbia St

Green St

Warren St

N 7th St

N 6th St

N 5th St

N 4th St

N 3rd St

N 2nd St

N 1st St

State St

Clinton St

Washington St

Prospect St

Columbia St

Union St

Partition St

Allen St

East Court St

Power Ave

Warren St

9
23
9
9
9
9
9G
23B
9
9G
23B

2
3
14
13
5
12
5
4
10
9
8
11
7
1
4
6
5
3
4
3
2
1
1
1
2
3
?
?

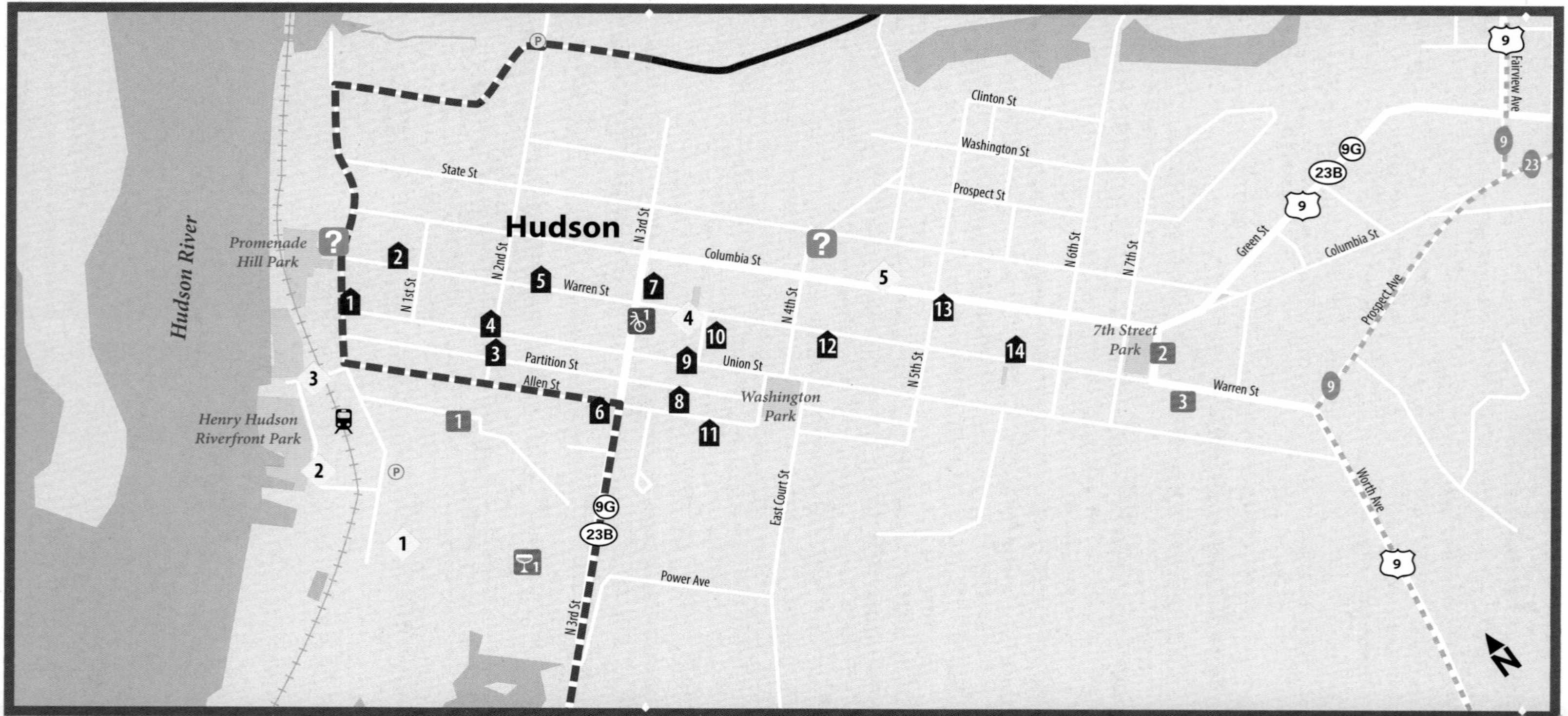

THINGS TO SEE & DO

1. Basilica Hudson — 110 South Front St. — (518) 822-1050
2. Hudson Paddles — 108 Water St. — (518) 992-5787
3. Hudson Cruises — 10 Ferry St. — (518) 822-1014
4. Hudson Hall — 327 Warren St. — (518) 822-1438
5. Time & Space Ltd. — 434 Columbia St. — (518) 822-8100

Warren Street in Hudson

TRAIL & TRAVEL NOTES

Antiques, Art and Cafes — Former New York City residents and a dynamic local population give Hudson a unique flair that has transformed it into a haven for the arts. Warren Street, the commercial heart of the city and a popular place for visitors to stroll, features many home design and antique shops, avant-garde galleries, clothing and jewelry boutiques, and eclectic eateries. For those looking for a fancy cocktail or coffee to sip, this is the place to stop.

Whale Tales — Visitors to Hudson may eye the friendly-faced whales on local street signs with curiosity. Their presence harkens to Hudson's past as a center of the American whaling industry. Hudson grew to prominence shortly after the Revolutionary War as a major port for trade and manufacturing, including a surprising concentration of whaling companies, given the city's distance from the ocean (the Hudson River is at sea level and navigable for commercial ships all the way from New York City to Albany). From the late eighteenth to the mid-nineteenth century, the population and wealth of the city grew, until the whaling trade collapsed. Hudson boasts a high number of properties on the National Historic Register, a testament to its former opulence.

VISITOR INFORMATION

Columbia County Tourism
401 State St.
(518) 828-3375
columbiacountytourism.org

AMENITIES

Hudson — 🌐 🛒 🍷 🍴 👫 ℞

A view of Hudson from Athens, circa 1820

65

MAP 16 - HUDSON - KINDERHOOK

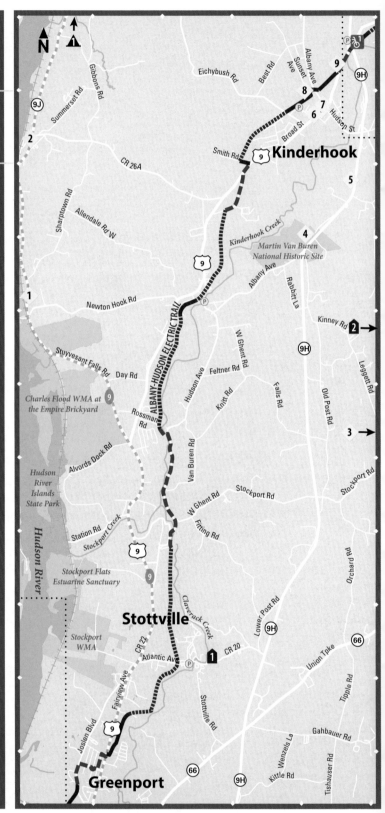

N

1 MILE

(9J)

2

Gibbons Rd

Summerset Rd

Eichybush Rd

Best Rd

Albany Ave

Sunset Ave

Hudson St

9

(9H)

8

7

6

Broad St

Smith Rd

9 **Kinderhook**

CR 26A

5

Sharptown Rd

Allendale Rd W

Kinderhook Creek

4

Martin Van Buren National Historic Site

Albany Ave

Rabbit La

9

Newton Hook Rd

Kinney Rd 2 →

ALBANY-HUDSON ELECTRIC TRAIL

Leggett Rd

Stuyvesant Falls Rd

Day Rd

W Ghent Rd

Feltner Rd

Falls Rd

(9H)

Old Post Rd

Charles Flood WMA at the Empire Brickyard

9

Hudson Ave

Knitt Rd

3 →

Rossman Rd

Stockport Rd

Alvords Dock Rd

Van Buren Rd

Stockport Rd

Hudson River Islands State Park

Orchard Rd

Station Rd

Stockport Creek

W Ghent Rd

9

Hudson River

Stockport Flats Estuarine Sanctuary

9

Fitting Rd

Stockport WMA

Lower Post Rd

(9H)

(66)

Stottville

Claverack Creek

CR 22

Atlantic Ave

1

CR 20

Union Tpke

Tipple Rd

Fairview Ave

Stottville Rd

Gahbauer Rd

Joslen Blvd

9

Wenzels La

Tishauser Rd

Kittle Rd

(66)

(9H)

Greenport

THINGS TO SEE & DO

1.	Stockport Flats & Historic Ice House	Ice House Rd.	(845) 889-4745
2.	Stuyvesant Railroad Station	81 Riverview St.	
3.	Art Omi Sculpture & Architecture Park	1405 County Rte. 22	(518) 392-4747
4.	Martin Van Buren National Historic Site	1012 Old Post Rd.	(518) 758-9689
5.	Ichabod Crane Schoolhouse	2598 NYS Rte. 9H	(518) 758-9265
	Luykas Van Alen House	2598 NYS Rte. 9H	(518) 758-9265
6.	Persons of Color Cemetery	15 Rothermel Ln.	(518) 758-9882
	Jack Shainman Gallery: The School	25 Broad St.	(518) 758-1628
7.	Columbia Co. Historical Society Museum & Library	5 Albany Ave.	(518) 758-9265
	James Vanderpoel 'House of History'	16 Broad St.	(518) 758-9265
8.	Samascott Orchards	5 Sunset Ave.	(518) 758-7224
9.	Samascott's Garden Market	65 Chatham St.	(518) 758-9292

TRAIL & TRAVEL NOTES

Vote for OK — Martin Van Buren, the eighth president of the United States, was born to a family of Dutch descent in Kinderhook. Educated as a lawyer, Van Buren rose through the ranks of New York State politics and went on to establish a political interest group known as the Albany Regency, which controlled state government for nearly two decades. During Van Buren's 1840 campaign for the presidency, he popularized the term "OK." While the etymology of the word has been disputed, and it was in use prior to the campaign, Van Buren used it at the time to mean "Old Kinderhook." Thus, a vote for OK was a vote for Van Buren.

Bucolic Landscapes — The trail runs alongside many active farms through Columbia County. Agriculture remains a vital part of the region's economy, and the tractors, equipment, sounds, and smells that are common on this stretch of the trail are a normal aspect of farming activities. Trail users should always be alert for farm equipment, stay on the trail, leave livestock undisturbed, and respect private property.

VISITOR INFORMATION

Columbia County Tourism
(518) 828-3375
columbiacountytourism.org

AMENITIES

Kinderhook

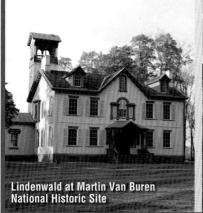

Lindenwald at Martin Van Buren National Historic Site

Scenic pastoral landscape between Kinderhook and Hudson

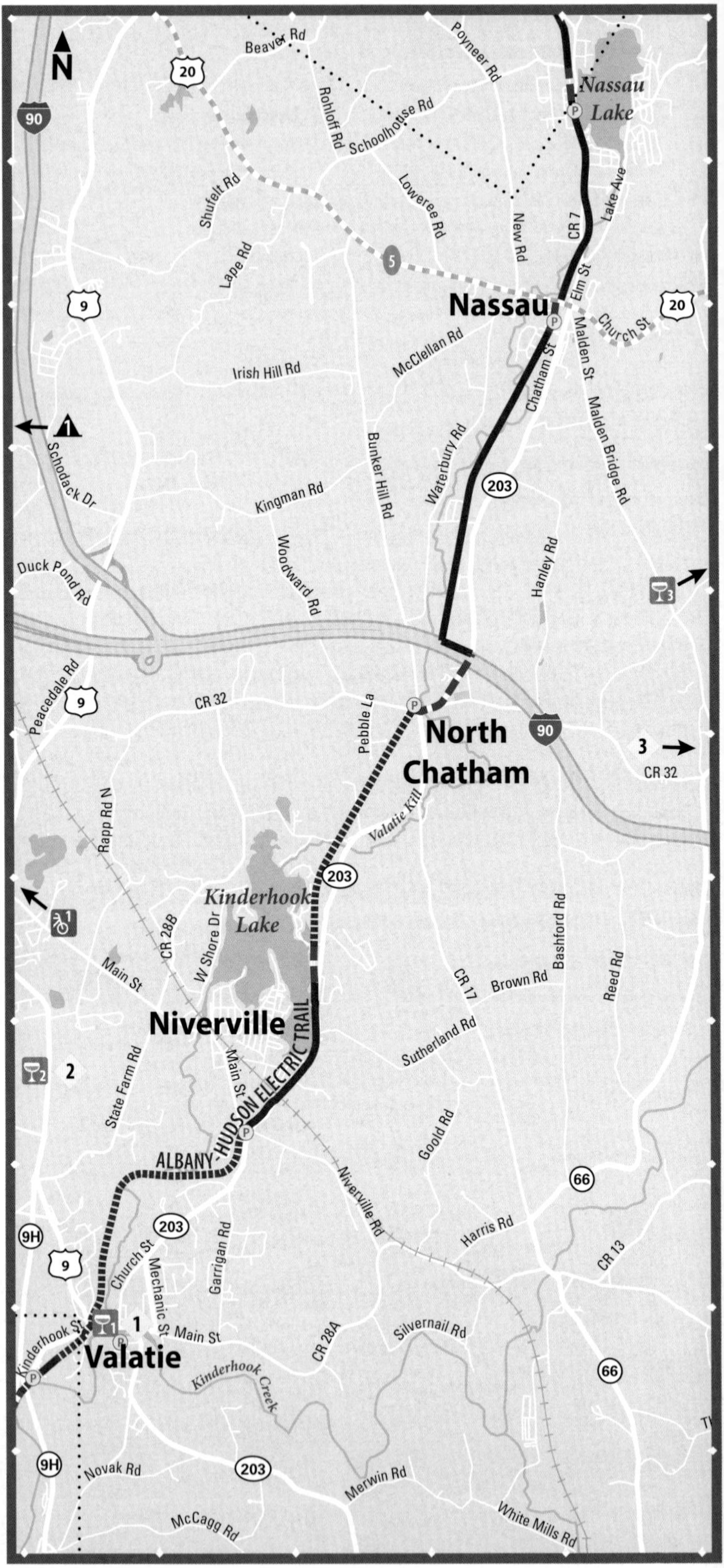

N

20

90

I MILE

9

Beaver Rd

Poyneer Rd

Nassau Lake

P

Rohloff Rd

Schoolhouse Rd

Shufelt Rd

Loweree Rd

New Rd

CR 7

Lake Ave

Lane Rd

5

20

Nassau

P

Elm St

Church St

20

Irish Hill Rd

McClellan Rd

Chatham St

Malden St

Malden Bridge Rd

Schodack Dr

Kingman Rd

Bunker Hill Rd

Waterbury Rd

203

Hanley Rd

Duck Pond Rd

CR 32

90

9

Peacedale Rd

Pebble La

P

North Chatham

3

CR 32

Rapp Rd N

Valatie Kill

203

Kinderhook Lake

CR 28B

Main St

Bashford Rd

State Farm Rd

2

Niverville

ALBANY–HUDSON ELECTRIC TRAIL

Main St

W Shore Dr

CR 17

Brown Rd

Reed Rd

Sutherland Rd

P

Goold Rd

66

9H

9

203

Church St

Garrigan Rd

Niverville Rd

Harris Rd

CR 13

Mechanic St

Main St

1

Valatie

Kinderhook St

P

CR 28A

Silvernail Rd

66

Kinderhook Creek

9H

Novak Rd

203

Merwin Rd

McCagg Rd

White Mills Rd

MAP 17   VALATIE - NASSAU

THINGS TO SEE & DO

1.	Valatie Community Theatre	3031 Main St.	(518) 758-1309
2.	Golden Harvest Farms	3074 US Rte. 9	(518) 758-7683
3.	Sabba Vineyard Estate	383 Pitts Rd.	(518) 766-3755

TRAIL & TRAVEL NOTES

"Little Falls" — Originally known to the Mohicans as Pachaquak, meaning "cleared meadow," Dutch settlers renamed the area Vaaltje, meaning "little falls," for the multiple small waterfalls of the Valatie Kill and Kinderhook Creek that surround the village.

Great Escape — Hungarian-born Harry Houdini moved to New York City with his family in 1887. As his magic career grew in fame, he began to make films, several of which were filmed in upstate New York. In 1921, Houdini filmed scenes of his silent adventure film, Haldane of the Secret Service, at Beaver Mills Falls on Kinderhook Creek. Beaver Cotton Mill Overlook is accessible from Main Street in Valatie and offers views of the falls, the creek, and Beaver Pond.

Albany-Hudson Electric Trail — Completed in 2020, the Albany-Hudson Electric Trail was one of the centerpieces of Hudson River Valley Greenway Trail development. The trail follows the route of the Albany & Hudson Electric Railway, a trolley that served communities between Albany and Hudson from 1899 to 1929. One of the most popular destinations along the route was "Electric Park," an amusement park on the shore of Kinderhook Lake.

VISITOR INFORMATION

Columbia County Tourism
(518) 828-3375
columbiacountytourism.org

Rensselaer County Tourism
(518) 270-2673
renscotourism.com

AMENITIES

Valatie   Rx

Nassau   Rx

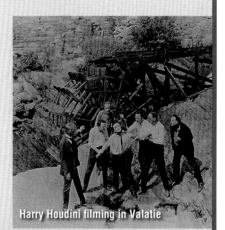
Harry Houdini filming in Valatie

Rolling through North Chatham

MAP 18   EAST GREENBUSH - RENSSELAER

1 MILE

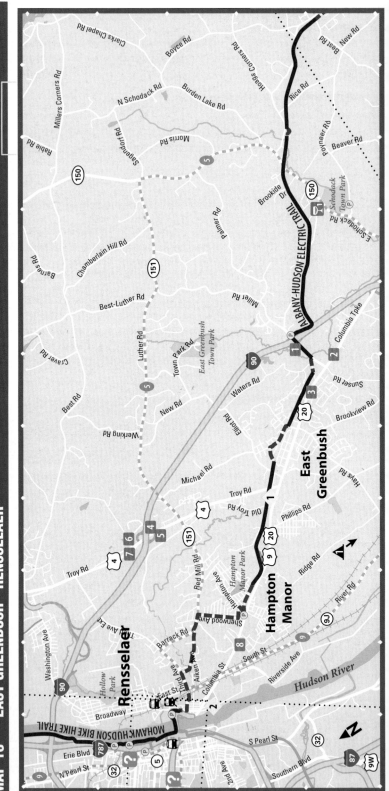

THINGS TO SEE & DO

1. Funplex Funpark   589 Columbia Turnpike   (518) 477-2651
2. Crailo State Historic Site   9 1/2 Riverside Ave.   (518) 463-8738

TRAIL & TRAVEL NOTES

Patroonships — The Dutch settled East Greenbush under the patroonship of Kiliaen van Rensselaer in 1630. The patroonship was a complex feudal system that created vast estates for the Dutch aristocracy who immigrated to New York, then known as New Netherland.

Reclamation — In 2021, 156 acres of land in East Greenbush were returned to the Stockbridge-Munsee Community Band of the Mohican Indians. The acreage comprises Papscanee Island, a forested nature preserve on the Hudson River with three miles of hiking trails. The preserve will continue to be protected and accessible to the public, and will be used for Mohican cultural events.

VISITOR INFORMATION

Rensselaer County Tourism
(518) 270-2673
renscotourism.com

AMENITIES

East Greenbush						R_x
Rensselaer						R_x

View of Albany skyline from Rensselaer

Crailo State Historic Site

71

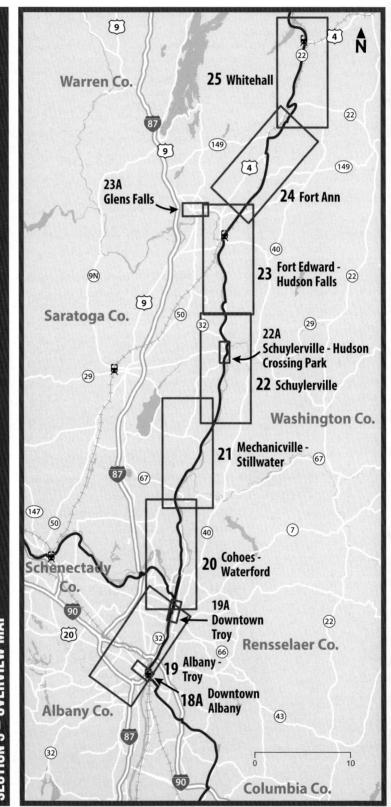

SECTION 3

ALBANY TO WHITEHALL

The southern half of the Champlain Valley Trail is also the northernmost segment of the Hudson River Valley Greenway Trail, connecting Albany to Whitehall. This 76-mile stretch is linked by the Mohawk-Hudson Bike-Hike Trail, the Champlain Canalway Trail, and sections of on-road riding along village streets, rural roads, and state highways. As of 2022, 50% of this section is off-road trails, welcoming bicyclists, walkers, and runners of all ages and abilities. The other half of the route, designated on the shoulders of public roads, is appropriate for experienced bicyclists comfortable riding adjacent to vehicle traffic (there are no designated bike lanes on the on-road sections).

The 11-mile section from Downtown Albany to Peebles Island State Park in Cohoes provides pleasant vistas of the Hudson River. Nine of the 11 miles are off-road paved trail, with two miles of on-road riding between Watervliet and Green Island. Riders can access Troy via a ramp up to the Route 378 bridge to South Troy, or by taking the Congress Street or Green Island Bridges in Watervliet or Green Island, respectively.

In Waterford, just north of Peebles Island State Park, riders pick up the Champlain Canalway Trail, which alternates between stone dust, paved surfaces, and on-road riding for 62 miles north to Whitehall. The first five miles from Waterford to Halfmoon is a stone dust trail, built on the towpath of the original Champlain Canal. The route then continues for 19 miles on-road from Halfmoon to Schuylerville. Cyclists should exercise caution on this portion of state highway, with traffic traveling at posted speeds of up to 55 mph.

In Schuylerville, an off-road trail is once again available, running a short distance along the towpath of the old Champlain Canal. A seasonal visitors center in Schuylerville provides some amenities. After Hudson Crossing Park, the route follows local low-traffic roads to Fort Miller. From Fort Miller to Fort Edward, riders share the road with higher speed traffic on U.S. Route 4.

At Fort Edward, the trail dips off-road onto a 12-mile dedicated off-road path, with a mix of paved and stone dust surfaces. This scenic section of the Champlain Canalway Trail concludes at Fort Ann. Riders continuing north follow rural, low-traffic roads for five miles to Comstock. The final eight miles from Comstock to Whitehall are on the shoulders of Route 4, a high-speed road with significant vehicle and truck traffic. The section between Fort Ann and Whitehall is not recommended for casual cyclists and is only suitable for those who are experienced and comfortable with on-road riding.

COMMUNITIES ALONG ROUTE

Albany County	Albany, Watervliet, Green Island, Cohoes
Rensselaer County	Troy
Saratoga County	Waterford, Mechanicville, Stillwater, Schuylerville
Washington County	Fort Edward, Hudson Falls, Glens Falls, Fort Ann, Whitehall

VISITOR INFORMATION

Albany County	discoveralbany.com	(518) 434-1217
Rensselaer County	renscotourism.com	(518) 270-2673
Saratoga County	saratoga.org	(518) 584-3255
Washington County	washingtoncounty.fun	(888) 203-8622

SAFETY & SECURITY

Universal Emergency Number: 911

Law Enforcement

State Police Troop G	Albany, Rensselaer, Saratoga & Washington Counties	(518) 783-3211
Albany County Sheriff	Albany	(518) 487-5400
Rensselaer County Sheriff	Troy	(518) 266-1900
Saratoga County Sheriff	Ballston Spa	(518) 885-6761
Washington County Sheriff	Fort Edward	(518) 746-2522

Walkers enjoying the Champlain Canalway Trail

TRANSPORTATION

Amtrak Rail Stations (800-USA-RAIL)   amtrak.com
Albany-Rensselaer (ALB)   525 East St.
Saratoga Springs (SAR)   26 Station Ln.
Fort Edward (FED)   70 East St.
Whitehall (WHL)   154 Main St.

Major Bus Stations
Greyhound Bus Terminal - Glens Falls   2 Hudson Ave.   (800) 858-8555
OurBus/Megabus - Rensselaer   525 East St.
Albany Bus Terminal   34 Hamilton St.   (518) 427-7060

Urban & Regional Transit
Capital District Transportation Authority   cdta.org   (518) 482-8822
Greater Glens Falls Transit   gftransit.org   (518) 792-1085

Commercial Airports
Albany International Airport   albanyairport.com   (518) 242-2222

HOSPITALS

Albany Medical Center Hospital	Albany	(518) 262-3125
Albany Memorial Hospital	Albany	(518) 471-3221
St. Peter's Hospital	Albany	(518) 525-1550
Samaritan Hospital	Troy	(518) 271-3300
St. Mary's Hospital	Troy	(518) 268-5000
Saratoga Hospital	Saratoga	(518) 587-3222
Glens Falls Hospital	Glens Falls	(518) 926-1000

On-road riding in Schuylerville

MAP 18A DOWNTOWN ALBANY

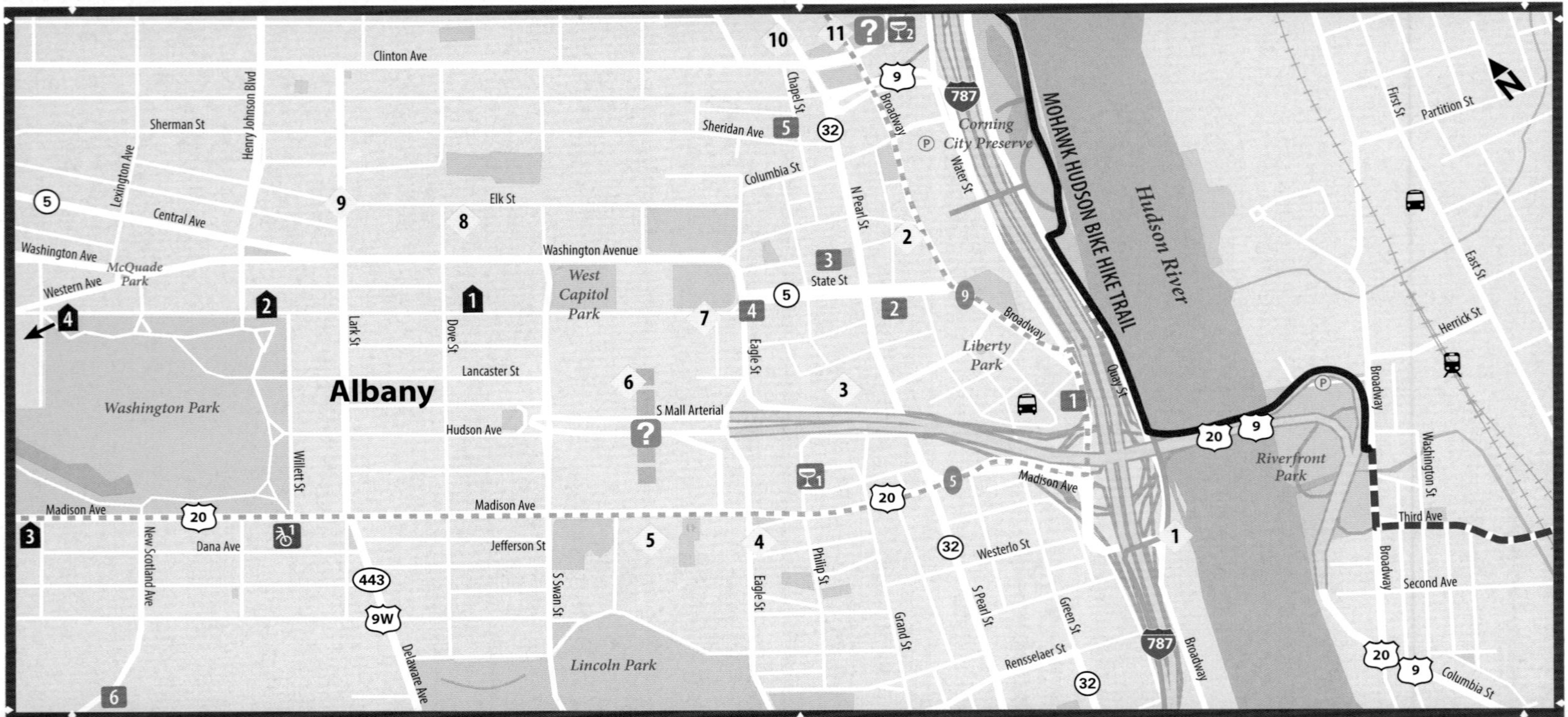

1 MILE

N

Hudson River

MOHAWK HUDSON BIKE HIKE TRAIL

Corning
City Preserve

Riverfront
Park

East St

First St

Partition St

Herrick St

Washington St

Third Ave

Second Ave

Columbia St

Broadway

Broadway

9

20

9

20

9

20

1

787

Broadway

787

Water St

Broadway

Broadway

9

Liberty Park

Quay St

1

32

Madison Ave

Green St

S Pearl St

Westerlo St

Rensselaer St

32

N Pearl St

State St

5

32

2

2

3

3

5

Grand St

20

9

11

10

Chapel St

Sheridan Ave

Columbia St

2

5

5

4

Eagle St

Eagle St

Philip St

4

32

7

S Mall Arterial

2

6

West Capitol
Park

Washington Avenue

5

S Swan St

Lincoln Park

Elk St

Lancaster St

Hudson Ave

Madison Ave

Jefferson St

Clinton Ave

8

1

Dove St

Albany

443

9W

Delaware Ave

9

Lark St

2

Henry Johnson Blvd

Willett St

20

Dana Ave

New Scotland Ave

Sherman St

Central Ave

Lexington Ave

McQuade Park

Washington Ave

Western Ave

Washington Park

Madison Ave

3

4

5

6

THINGS TO SEE & DO

1.	Destroyer Escort U.S.S. Slater	141 Broadway	(518) 431-1943
2.	Albany Center Gallery	488 Broadway	(518) 462-4775
3.	MVP Arena	51 South Pearl St.	(518) 487-2000
4.	Executive Mansion	138 Eagle St.	(518) 474-2418
	Cathedral of the Immaculate Conception	125 Eagle St.	(518) 463-4447
5.	The Egg Center for the Performing Arts	Empire State Plaza	(518) 473-1845
	New York State Museum	222 Madison Ave.	(518) 474-5877
6.	Empire State Plaza	100 S Mall Arterial	(518) 474-2418
7.	New York State Capitol	Washington Ave. & State St.	(518) 474-8860
8.	Albany Institute of History and Art	125 Washington Ave.	(518) 463-4478
9.	Lark Street	Washington Ave. to Madison Ave.	(518) 415-1109
10.	Palace Theatre	19 Clinton Ave.	(518) 465-3335
11.	Irish American Heritage Museum	21 Quackenbush Sq.	(518) 427-1916

Albany's famous tulips recall the city's Dutch heritage

TRAIL & TRAVEL NOTES

State Capitol — Completed in 1899 after nearly 30 years and a cost of $25 million, several prominent architects, including Henry Hobson Richardson, contributed to the mix of styles of this architecturally unique building. The State Senate Chamber is one of the most ornate legislative chambers in the country, reflecting the style and symbolizing the wealth and prominence of New York State during the "Gilded Age." Guided tours showcase the building interior, which has been extensively restored to its historic grandeur.

Empire State Plaza — This huge state office complex is an architectural feature itself, but also boasts an important collection of twentieth century paintings and sculpture. The New York State Museum, at the opposite end of the public plaza from the Capitol, features permanent exhibits about New York's history and culture and hosts temporary fine art and cultural exhibits.

Empire State Plaza

VISITOR INFORMATION

Discover Albany
25 Quackenbush Sq.
(518) 434-1217
albany.org

AMENITIES

Albany   🍴 🛒 ⛽ 🚻 Rx

1 MILE

MAP 19   ALBANY - TROY

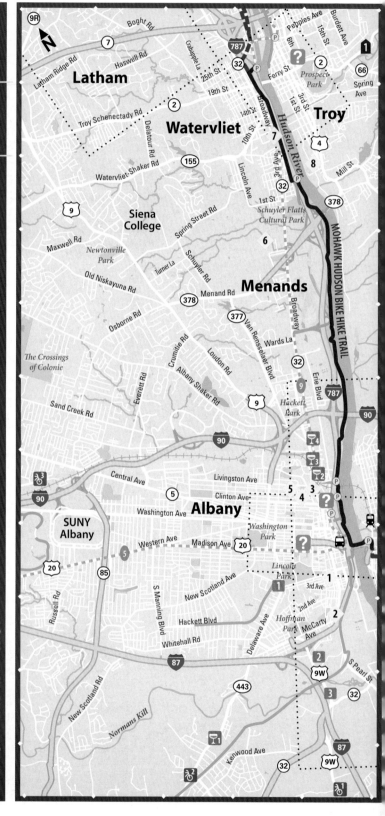

THINGS TO SEE & DO

1.	Schuyler Mansion State Historic Site	32 Catherine St.	(518) 434-0835
2.	Historic Cherry Hill	523 1/2 South Pearl St.	(518) 434-4791
3.	Capital Repertory Theater	251 North Pearl St.	(518) 462-4531
4.	Ten Broeck Mansion	9 Ten Broeck Pl.	(518) 436-9826
5.	Underground Railroad Education Center	194 Livingston Ave.	(518) 621-7793
6.	Albany Rural Cemetery	3 Cemetery Ave.	(518) 463-7017
7.	Watervliet Arsenal	1 Buffington St.	(518) 266-5111
8.	Burden Iron Works Museum	1 East Industrial Pkwy.	(518) 274-5267

TRAIL & TRAVEL NOTES

What's Brewing — North Albany's warehouse district, once home to the city's lumber industry, now features several breweries, distilleries, and a cidery. Many of these local craft beverage makers have tasting rooms located just a short ride away from the trail which runs through Albany's Corning Waterfront Preserve.

Livingston Avenue Bridge — Visitors to Corning Waterfront Preserve will note the rotating swing bridge over the Hudson, connecting Albany and Rensselaer. The bridge was constructed in 1902, on stone supports from an earlier pre-Civil War iteration. In prior decades, the bridge included a pedestrian walkway that has since been closed due to safety concerns. A grassroots effort, the Livingston Avenue Bridge Coalition, has been advocating since 2012 for the restoration of the walkway on a new or rebuilt structure to restore bike and pedestrian access across the Hudson at this location.

Albany Rural Cemetery — This pastoral cemetery is considered one of the most picturesque in the country, with over 400 acres of rolling hills, stately trees, and beautifully crafted nineteenth century monuments. Significant residents of Albany Rural Cemetery include Chester A. Arthur, the 21st President of the United States, Alice Morgan Wright, a sculptor, women's suffragist, and animal welfare advocate, and members of the Corning family, founders of the New York Central Railroad and an influential Albany political dynasty.

VISITOR INFORMATION

Discover Albany
(800) 258-3582
albany.org

Rensselaer County Tourism
(518) 270-2673
renscotourism.com

Find out what's on tap at the tasting rooms in North Albany

1 MILE

Green Island

Tibbits Ave

Bleeker St

Arch St

Canal St

James St

Paine St

George St

Hudson Ave

Lower Hudson Ave Park

787

7

Paine St

Maplewood Historic Park

Albany Ave

25th St

32

24th St

787

23rd St

2nd Ave

21st St

2

18th St

16th St

Watervliet Veterans Memorial Park

15th St

2nd Ave

14th St

Watervliet

13th St   32

155

MOHAWK HUDSON BIKE HIKE TRAIL

9

Green Island Bridge

Lower Hudson Ave

P

9

Hudson River

Hudson Shores Park

River St

19th St

6th Ave

Ingalls Ave

4

Middleburgh St

9

River St

5th Ave

Hoosick St

8th St

9th St

7

7

6th Ave

6th Avenue Park

2

1   Hutton St

4

2

Jacob St

Peoples Ave

P   Federal St

1   4th St

William D. Chamberlain Riverfront Park   Fulton St

2   3rd St   Broadway   6th Ave   7

River St   State St

3   2nd St   8th St

1st St   6

4   Congress St   2

1   5th St

Ferry St

Sage Park   2

5   **Troy**

Division St

Liberty St

River St   Washington St   4

Washington Park   4

Adams St   3rd St   4th St

Jefferson St

Ida St

Canal Ave   *Poesten Kill*

Prospect Park

Hill St

N

THINGS TO SEE & DO

1.	River Street	Third St. to Congress St.	(518) 279-7997
2.	Arts Center of the Capital Region	265 River St.	(518) 273-0552
3.	Troy Savings Bank Music Hall	30 2nd St.	(518) 273-0038
4.	Hart-Cluett Museum	57 2nd St.	(518) 272-7232
5.	Russell Sage College	65 1st St.	(518) 244-2000
6.	Experimental Media and Performing Arts Center	44 8th St.	(518) 276-3921
7.	Rensselaer Polytechnic Institute	110 8th St.	(518) 276-6000

TRAIL & TRAVEL NOTES

Gilded Age — At the end of the nineteenth century, Troy was one of the wealthiest cities in America. A ride through downtown to the Washington Park neighborhood offers a visual feast of grand Victorian-era architecture, with finely detailed wood, stone, and iron work. Several of Troy's churches feature stained-glass windows created by Louis Comfort Tiffany. The downtown area has been used to film several major movies and TV series set in the Gilded Age. The inequity between the vast wealth of factory owners and the hard work and low pay of their employees at the time inspired the formation of unions, including the first female labor union in the country.

Underground Railroad — In 1860, the abolitionist citizens of Troy, alongside Harriet Tubman, engaged in an elaborate and dangerous rescue mission on behalf of Charles Nalle, a formerly enslaved man who was captured by the authorities. In a wild street scene, abolitionists wrenched Nalle away from law enforcement and headed down the Hudson River, where they were apprehended. Tubman and her compatriots managed to free Nalle a second time, whisking him away to Western New York until they could raise enough funds to buy his freedom. A plaque on the corner of 1st and State Streets commemorates the rescue.

Out On the Town — Troy's nightlife scene is lively and cultured, with many art galleries, bars, restaurants, and venues to see live performances.

VISITOR INFORMATION

Rensselaer County Tourism
1600 7th Ave.
(518) 270-2673
renscotourism.com

AMENITIES

Troy

Troy Savings Bank Music Hall

View of Troy from the Hedley Building

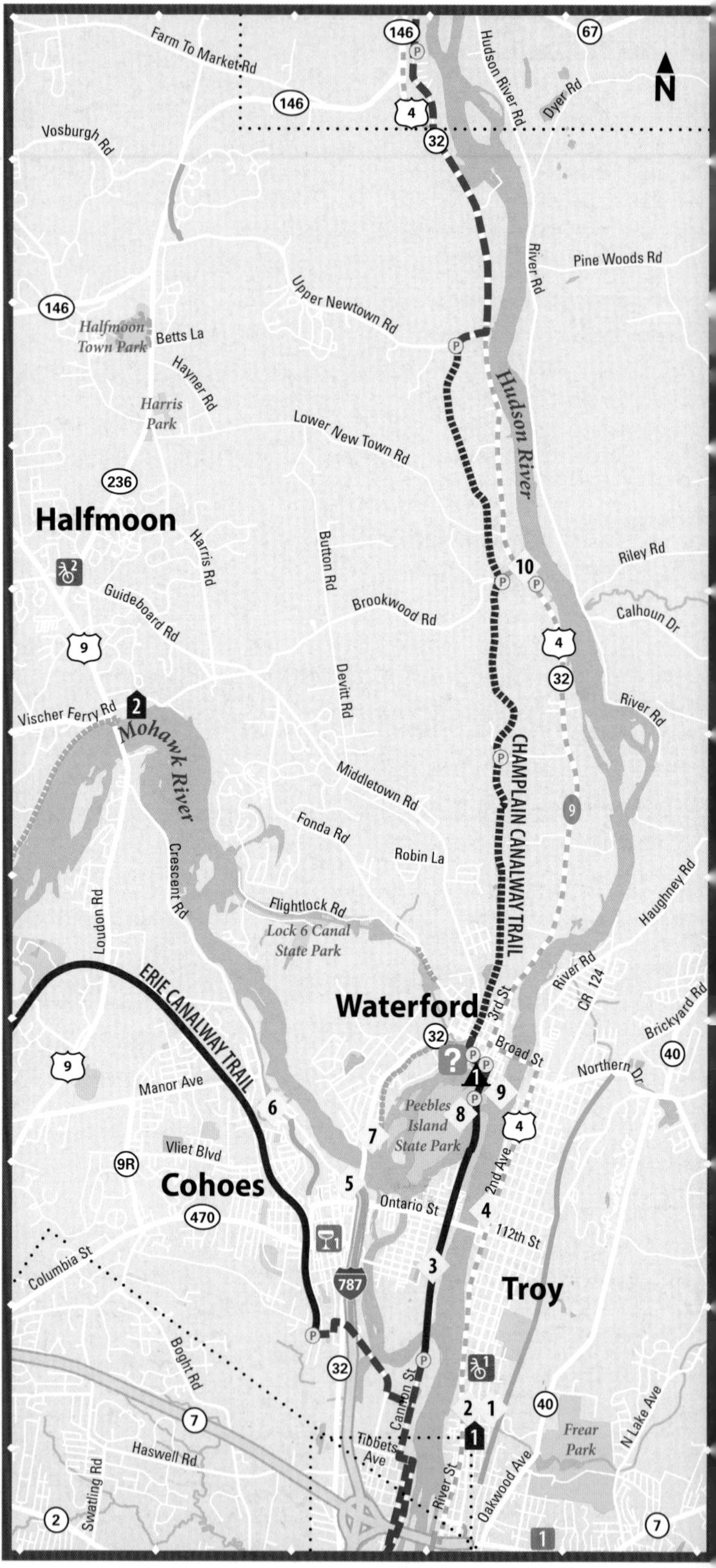

MAP 20   COHOES - WATERFORD

N

Farm To Market Rd

(146)

(67)

Hudson River Rd

4

Dyer Rd

32

Vosburgh Rd

River Rd

Pine Woods Rd

(146)

Halfmoon
Town Park

Betts La

Upper Newtown Rd

Hayner Rd

Harris
Park

Lower New Town Rd

Hudson River

(236)

Halfmoon

Harris Rd

Button Rd

Brookwood Rd

Riley Rd

10

Calhoun Dr

2

4

Guideboard Rd

9

Devitt Rd

32

River Rd

Vischer Ferry Rd

2

Mohawk River

Middletown Rd

9

CHAMPLAIN CANALWAY TRAIL

Loudon Rd

Crescent Rd

Fonda Rd

Robin La

Haughney Rd

Flightlock Rd

Lock 6 Canal
State Park

River Rd

CR 124

Brickyard Rd

ERIE CANALWAY TRAIL

Waterford

32

Broad St

40

9

?

1

Northern Dr

9

Manor Ave

6

Peebles
Island
State Park

8

9

4

2nd Ave

Vliet Blvd

7

(9R)

Cohoes

5

Ontario St

(470)

1

4

112th St

787

3

Troy

Columbia St

32

Canion St

1

Bogbt Rd

7

Haswell Rd

Tibbets
Ave

River St

2 1

1

Oakwood Ave

40

Frear
Park

N Lake Ave

(2)

Swatling Rd

1

(7)

THINGS TO SEE & DO

1.	Oakwood Cemetery	50 101st St.	(518) 272-7520
2.	The Sanctuary for Independent Media	3361 6th Ave.	(518) 272-2390
3.	The Van Schaick Mansion	1 Van Schaick Ave.	(518) 489-5160
4.	Lansingburgh Historical Society & Herman Melville House	2 114th St.	(518) 235-3501
5.	Cohoes Music Hall	58 Remsen St.	(518) 434-0776
6.	Cohoes Falls Overlook and Falls View Park	231-341 N Mohawk St.	(518) 743-2080
7.	Waterford Historical Museum and Cultural Center	2 Museum Ln.	(518) 238-0809
8.	Peebles Island State Park	1 Delaware Ave. N	(518) 268-2188
9.	Upstate Kayak Rentals	1st St. & Front St.	(518) 209-1063
10.	Halfmoon Lighthouse Park	597 Hudson River Rd.	(518) 371-7410

TRAIL & TRAVEL NOTES

Cohoes Falls — Cohoes Falls is a significant cultural, historical, and ecological landmark. To the Haudenosaunee confederacy, the waterfall is a sacred place where The Great Peacemaker persuaded the Mohawk to bring together the five nations of Indigenous people in the region into one federation. The impressive waterfall spans 1,000 feet and drops as much as 90 feet, comparable in width to the American side of Niagara Falls. Lucky visitors to the Cohoes Falls Overlook and Falls View Park will spot the freewheeling flight of bald eagles, which nest nearby.

Peebles Island State Park — Trails around the rocky cliffs of this channel island give a unique perspective of the powerful erosive force of the Mohawk River at its confluence with the Hudson River. The park contains the remains of Revolutionary War earthworks, constructed to halt the British advance on Albany, and the Matton Shipyard, which built wooden boats and steel tugboats for use on the Erie and Champlain Canals.

Tugboat Fun — The Tugboat Roundup is an annual gathering of tugboats, workboats and barges that celebrates the maritime heritage of the Northeast Inland Waterways. The September festival features boat tours, rides, and competitions, a tugboat parade, fireworks, children's activities, vendors, food, and more.

VISITOR INFORMATION

Discover Albany
(800) 258-3582
albany.org

Discover Saratoga
(518) 584-1531
discoversaratoga.org

Waterford Harbor Visitor Center
1 Tugboat Alley
(518) 233-9123
town.waterford.ny.us

AMENITIES

Cohoes	🅟 🛒 👕 👚 👫 Rx
Waterford	🅟 👕 👚 👫

Riding across the Mohawk River to Peebles Island

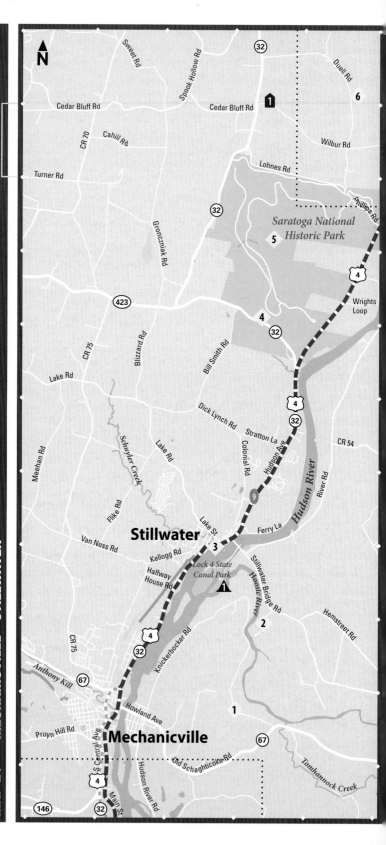

N

1 MILE

Sweet Rd

Spook Hollow Rd

32

Duell Rd

6

Cedar Bluff Rd

Cedar Bluff Rd

1

Wilbur Rd

CR 70

Cahill Rd

Lohnes Rd

Turner Rd

Phillips Rd

32

Saratoga National
Historic Park

5

4

Gronczniak Rd

423

4

32

Blizzard Rd

Bill Smith Rd

4

CR 75

Lake Rd

Dick Lynch Rd

Schuyler Creek

Lake Rd

Stratton La

Colonial Rd

Hudson Ave

CR 54

Meehan Rd

Fiike Rd

4

32

Hudson River

River Rd

9

Van Ness Rd

Lake St

Stillwater

3

Ferry La

Kellogg Rd

Lock 4 State
Canal Park

Halfway
House Rd

2

Stillwater Bridge Rd

Hoosic River

Hemstreet Rd

Knickerbocker Rd

4

32

Anthony Kill

67

Howland Ave

1

Pruyn Hill Rd

Mechanicville

67

CR 75

US Central Ave

Old Schaghticoke Rd

Tomhannock Creek

4

Main St

Hudson River Rd

146

32

Wrights
Loop

THINGS TO SEE & DO

1.	Knickerbocker Mansion	132 Knickerbocker Rd.	(518) 664-1700
2.	Liberty Ridge Farm	29 Bevis Rd.	(518) 664-1515
3.	Stillwater Blockhouse	692 Hudson Ave.	(518) 664-6148
4.	Saratoga National Historical Park	648 NYS Rte. 32	(518) 670-2985
5.	Neilson Farm	Saratoga Nat'l Hist. Pk.	(518) 670-2985
6.	Gerald B.H. Solomon Saratoga National Cemetery	200 Duell Rd.	(518) 581-9128

TRAIL & TRAVEL NOTES

The Battles of Saratoga — Saratoga National Historical Park preserves the site of the first major American military victory of the American Revolutionary War. The Battles of Saratoga in 1777 were a crucial turning point that led France to recognize the independence of the United States and enter the fight as an ally to the Americans. The park features over 3,000 acres of land to explore and great cycling opportunities, with multiple historic sites and exhibits in the Visitors Center.

The "Mechanical Arts" — Mechanicville was named after its population of craftspeople working in production trades. As railways were laid through the city and a hydroelectric power plant built, Mechanicville became a commercial hub during the Second Industrial Revolution, also known as the Technological Revolution. As railroads declined, so did the commercial importance of the area. The Mechanicville Hydroelectric Plant is currently the oldest continuously operating plant of its kind in the United States.

VISITOR INFORMATION

Rensselaer County Tourism
(518) 270-2673
renscotourism.com

Discover Saratoga
(518) 584-1531
discoversaratoga.org

AMENITIES

Mechanicville

Stillwater

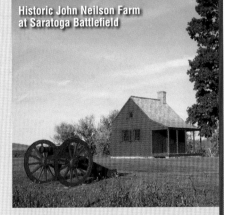
Historic John Neilson Farm at Saratoga Battlefield

A revolutionary war re-enactment at Saratoga National Historical Park

MAP 22   SCHUYLERVILLE

THINGS TO SEE & DO

1.	Saratoga Surrender Site	US Rte. 4 at Schuyler St.	(518) 670-2985
2.	Saratoga Clay Arts Center	167 Hayes Rd.	(518) 581-2529
3.	Washington County Fairgrounds	392 Old Schuylerville Rd.	(518) 692-2464
4.	Saratoga Monument	Burgoyne St.	(518) 670-2985
5.	Denton Wildlife Sanctuary	138 US Rte. 4	(518) 690-7878

TRAIL & TRAVEL NOTES

Garments for Change — Ellen Curtis Demorest, a Schuylerville native, was a fashion designer and women's rights advocate who created the first mass-marketed paper pattern for the construction of clothing. Demorest set up her first millinery shop in Saratoga Springs in 1842. She went on to move her business to Troy, and then to New York City. She later began a magazine which featured her new innovation—a paper pattern—stapled into each copy. The patterns were a runaway success, and she sold millions. Demorest championed many reform issues, including women's equality, using the hugely popular magazine as a platform.

Champlain Canalway Trail — The 7-mile portion of the Champlain Canalway Trail running from Schuylerville to Fort Miller includes a mix of off- and on-road travel. After passing the Visitor Center in the Village of Schuylerville, the section through Hudson Crossing Park to the Dix Bridge follows the stone dust towpath of the nineteenth century Champlain Canal. From there, the route travels along local roads north for just over five miles to Fort Miller, passing by woods, farmlands, and the active Champlain Canal, and featuring scenic river views. These low-traffic roads are comfortable for walkers and casual bicyclists.

VISITOR INFORMATION

Discover Saratoga
(518) 584-1531
discoversaratoga.org

Ellen Curtis Demorest

Saratoga Battlefield in autumn

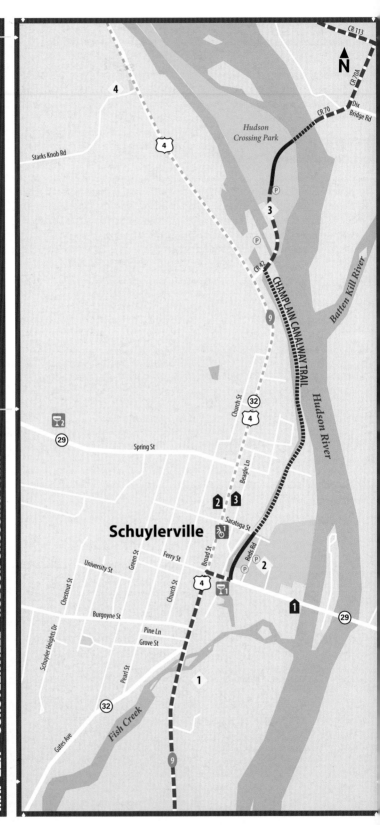

1 MILE

N

CR 113

CR 70A

CR 70

Dix
Bridge Rd

4

*Hudson
Crossing Park*

Starks Knob Rd

4

P

3

P

CR 42

CHAMPLAIN CANALWAY TRAIL

9

Batten Kill River

Hudson River

Church St

32

4

29

Spring St

Beagle Ln

2 3

Schuylerville

Saratoga St

1

Ferry St

Green St

University St

Broad St

Church St

Reds Rd

P

P 2

4

1

29

Chestnut St

Burgoyne St

Pine Ln

Grove St

Schuyler Heights Dr

1

Pearl St

32

Gates Ave

Fish Creek

9

THINGS TO SEE & DO

1. General Philip Schuyler House   4 Broad St.   (518) 670-2985
2. Fort Hardy Park   1 Reds Rd.   (518) 695-3881
3. Hudson Crossing Park   County Rte. 42   (518) 350-7275
4. Stark's Knob   Starks Knob Rd.

TRAIL & TRAVEL NOTES

Country Estate — Traveling north on Route 4, just before the bridge over Fish Creek, is the General Phillip Schuyler House. The Schuylers were a prominent early Dutch family. The family's first farm was destroyed in 1745 in a conflict with French Canadians and Indigenous people that left Philip Schuyler's father dead. In 1777, the property was destroyed a second time by retreating British forces after the Battles of Saratoga. The current historic home, rebuilt again in 1777, has hosted famous guests such as George Washington, Alexander Hamilton, Thomas Jefferson, and James Madison.

Hudson Crossing Park — Hudson Crossing Park is named for its historical and geographic location—Indigenous people used the area as a crossing point for thousands of years, and it was used strategically by the American military during the Revolutionary War. Today, the year-round park offers visitors more than two miles of nature trails with panoramic Hudson River views, picnic facilities, fishing and birding sites, art installations, a children's play garden, and a kayak launch.

VISITOR INFORMATION

Discover Saratoga
(518) 584-1531
discoversaratoga.org

AMENITIES

Schuylerville

General Philip Schuyler House

Riding across the Dix Bridge in Hudson Crossing Park

MAP 23   FORT EDWARD - HUDSON FALLS

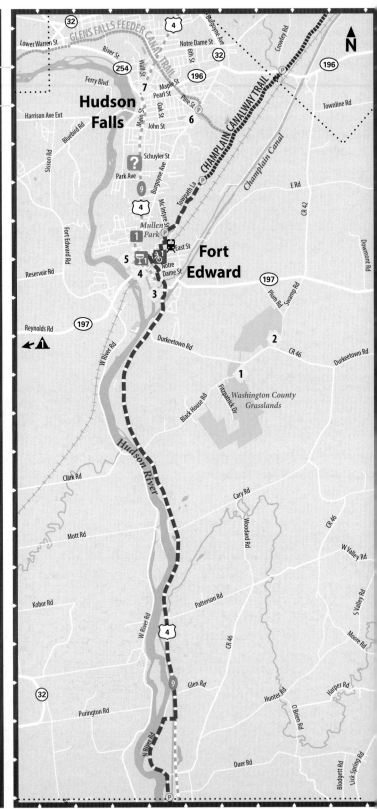

1 MILE

N

Lower Warren St
GLENS FALLS FEEDER CANAL TRAIL
32
4
Burgoyne Ave
Crowley Rd
Notre Dame St
River St
6th St
32
196
254
Wall St
Ferry Blvd
Maple St
7
196
Townline Rd
Harrison Ave Ext
Pearl St
Pine St
Bluebird Rd
Oak St
6
Hudson
Falls
Sisson Rd
John St
Main St
CHAMPLAIN CANALWAY TRAIL
Champlain Canal
E Rd
CR 42
Fort Edward Rd
Schuyler St
Park Ave
?
9
Burgoyne Ave
Towpath La
Downont Rd
4
Mc Intyre St
Reservoir Rd
Mullen
Park
P
East St
1
Fort
Edward
197
Plum Rd
Swamp Rd
5
4
Notre
Dame St
3
Reynolds Rd
197
W River Rd
Durkeetown Rd
2
CR 46
Durkeetown Rd
1
Washington County
Grasslands
Fitzpatrick Dr
Black House Rd
Clark Rd
Cary Rd
Woodard Rd
CR 46
Mott Rd
W Valley Rd
Kobor Rd
Patterson Rd
S Valley Rd
Moore Rd
Hudson River
4
CR 46
Hunter Rd
O Brien Rd
Harper Rd
32
Glen Rd
Purington Rd
9
N River Rd
Duer Rd
Blodgett Rd
Lick Spring Rd
W M River Rd
P

THINGS TO SEE & DO

1.	Washington County Grasslands Wildlife Sanctuary	390 Black House Rd.	(518) 897-1291
2.	Little Theater on the Farm	27 Plum Rd.	(518) 747-3421
3.	Old Fort House Museum	29 Broadway	(518) 747-9600
4.	Rogers Island	11 Rogers Island Dr.	(518) 747-3693
5.	Washington County Historical Society	167 Broadway	(518) 747-9108
6.	The Five Combines	Burgoyne Ave.	(518) 792-5363
7.	Strand Theater	210 Main St.	(518) 832-3484
	Broadway Upstate	132 Main St.	(518) 409-8463

TRAIL & TRAVEL NOTES

Historic Charm and Modern Art — The village of Hudson Falls features a significant central historic district, with nearly 150 buildings built between 1812 and 1935 in an assortment of architectural styles. Recently, a resurgence of arts and entertainment venues has revitalized the downtown area.

Rogers Island — Rogers Island, located in the Hudson River and part of the town of Fort Edward, has a rich history. Artifacts found there date back 6,000 years to when the island was part of Haudenosaunee territory. In the eighteenth century, Rogers Island and Fort Edward became a British fortress during the French and Indian War. The fortress was the third largest "city" in colonial North America at the time. Though it was evacuated prior to the American Revolutionary War, the island was again inhabited during the nineteenth century by soldiers in training for the Civil War. The Rogers Island Visitors Center and the Old Fort House Museum are excellent places to learn more about the area's history.

VISITOR INFORMATION

Painting of Fort Edward, circa 1820

Washington County
383 Broadway
(888) 203-8622
washingtoncounty.fun

AMENITIES

Fort Edward	🍴 🛒 🥡 👕	Rx
Hudson Falls	🍴 🛒 🥡 👕	Rx

The Five Combines in Kingsbury, along the Glens Falls Feeder Canal

1 MILE

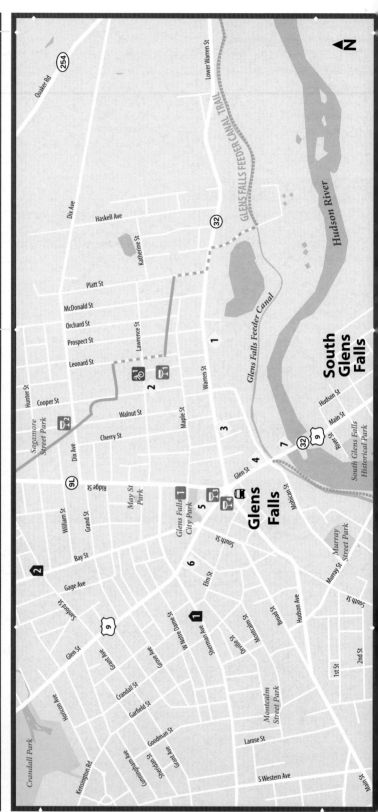

N

Quaker Rd

254

Dix Ave

Haskell Ave

Katherine St

Lower Warren St

GLENS FALLS FEEDER CANAL TRAIL

32

Platt St

McDonald St

Orchard St

Prospect St

Leonard St

Lawrence St

Hudson River

Glens Falls Feeder Canal

1

Warren St

2

Hunter St

Cooper St

Sagamore Street Park

Walnut St

Cherry St

Maple St

3

South Glens Falls

Hudson St

Main St

Bay St

Main St

River St

32

9

South Glens Falls Historical Park

7

4

Glen St

Dix Ave

9L

Ridge St

May St Park

Glens Falls City Park

1

3

4

5

Glens Falls

Mohican St

William St

Grand St

South St

6

Elm St

Murray St

Murray Street Park

Gage Ave

2

Sanford St

Glen St

9

Grant Ave

Grove Ave

Crandall St

Garfield St

Goodman St

Grant Ave

W Notre Dame St

Orville St

Montcalm St

1

Sherman Ave

Broad St

Hudson Ave

Montcalm Street Park

South St

Larose St

1st St

2nd St

S Western Ave

Main St

Horicon Ave

Kensington Rd

Cunningham Ave

Sheffield St

Crandall Park

THINGS TO SEE & DO

1.	Hyde Collection Art Museum and Historic House	161 Warren St.	(518) 792-1761
2.	The Shirt Factory	71 Lawrence St.	(518) 502-1450
3.	World Awareness Children's Museum	89 Warren St.	(518) 793-2773
4.	Cool Insuring Arena - Adirondack Thunder Hockey	1 Civic Center Plaza	(518) 798-0366
5.	LARAC Lapham Gallery	7 Lapham Pl.	(518) 798-1144
	Folklife Center at Crandall Public Library	251 Glen St.	(518) 792-6508
	Charles R. Wood Theater	207 Glen St.	(518) 480-4878
6.	Chapman Museum	348 Glen St.	(518) 793-2826
7.	Cooper's Cave Overlook	Cooper's Cave Bridge	

Downtown Glens Falls

TRAIL & TRAVEL NOTES

Novel Attraction — Inspired by a trip through the Adirondacks in 1825, James Fenimore Cooper set his classic American novel *The Last of the Mohicans* in locations across Washington County. The main character, Hawkeye, hides with his companions in what is now known as Cooper's Cave. Visitors to Glens Falls can experience the mystery of the cave for themselves, at the Cooper's Cave Overlook.

"Hometown U.S.A." — Glens Falls was once called Chepontuc, a Mohawk word meaning "hard place to get around," due to the nearby waterfall in the Hudson River. Glens Falls rapidly industrialized in the nineteenth century. The paper industry boomed due to the close proximity of the Hudson River and Adirondack forests, and is still an important part of the local economy. Glens Falls was famously called "Hometown U.S.A." by Look Magazine in 1944 for its small-town charm and easy access to urban conveniences.

Glens Falls Feeder Canal — The original Champlain Canal opened to boat traffic in 1822, providing direct access for freight and passenger boats from Lake Champlain at Whitehall to the Hudson River north of Albany. This created an important inland route from the St. Lawrence River to the docks of New York City. A "feeder canal" was built to supply water from the Hudson River at Glens Falls to the highest point on the Champlain Canal near Fort Edward. Boat traffic on the Feeder Canal ceased in 1928 but the remains of the canal and its adjacent towpath, restored for public use, provide recreational opportunities and a glimpse into the past.

VISITOR INFORMATION

Washington County
(888) 203-8622
washingtoncounty.fun

AMENITIES

Glens Falls

1 MILE

MAP 24   FORT ANN

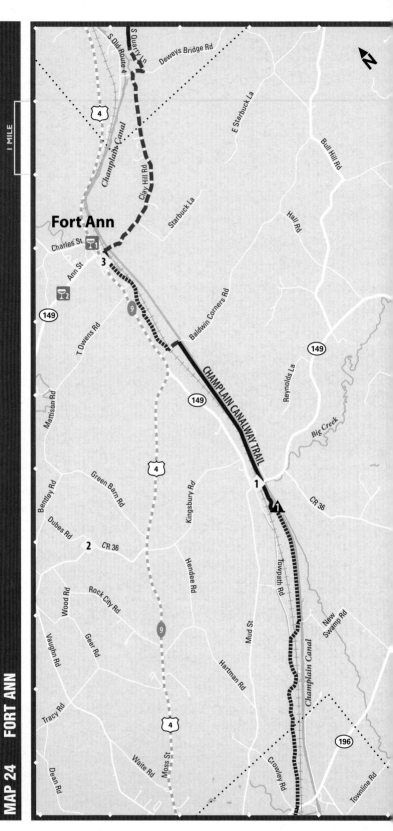

N

S Quarry Ln

S Old Route 4

Deweys Bridge Rd

4

Champlain Canal

City Hill Rd

E Starbuck La

Bull Hill Rd

Starbuck La

Fort Ann

Charles St

Ann St

149

T Owens Rd

Hall Rd

Baldwin Corners Rd

149

CHAMPLAIN CANALWAY TRAIL

Reynolds La

149

Big Creek

Mattison Rd

Green Barn Rd

4

Kingsbury Rd

1

CR 36

Bentley Rd

Dubes Rd

CR 36

Hendee Rd

Towpath Rd

New Swamp Rd

Wood Rd

Rock City Rd

9

Mud St

Vaughn Rd

Geer Rd

Hartman Rd

Champlain Canal

Tracy Rd

4

196

Dean Rd

Waite Rd

Moss St

Crowley Rd

Townline Rd

THINGS TO SEE & DO

1.	Champlain Canal Lock 9	2450 NYS Rte. 149	(518) 747-6021
2.	Red Wagon Farm	1 Dubes Rd.	(518) 889-2466
3.	Old Stone House Library	36 George St.	(518) 639-4071

TRAIL & TRAVEL NOTES

The Queen's Fort — The Fort Ann area has hosted several forts, from a French encampment near the southern end of Lake Champlain to a series of garrisons, including "Fort Schuyler" and the "Queen's Fort." The latter, renamed Fort Anne in the early 1700s after the Queen of the British Empire (the "e" in the town's name has been lost over the years), was destroyed and rebuilt several times. In the American Revolution, the Battle of Fort Anne was a loss for the colonists, who were in retreat from the British army at Fort Ticonderoga. However, strategic choices made at the battle led to later success in defeating the British at the Battles of Saratoga.

VISITOR INFORMATION

Washington County
(888) 203-8622
washingtoncounty.fun

AMENITIES

Fort Ann

Map of John Burgoyne's 1777
Campaign and the Battle of Fort Anne ▶

The Champlain Canalway Trail
just outside of Fort Ann

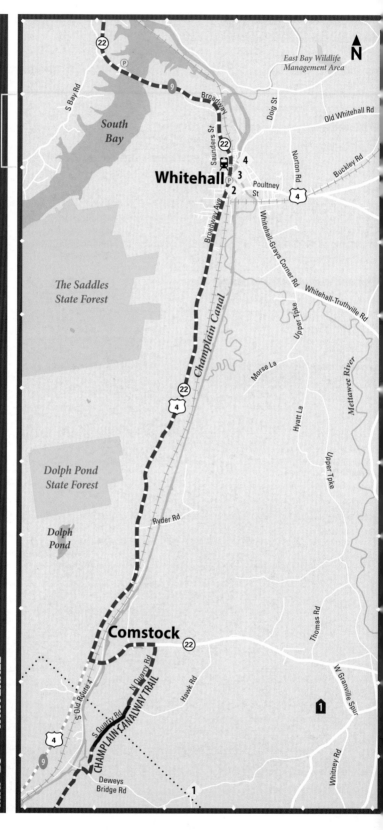

MAP 25   WHITEHALL

THINGS TO SEE & DO

1.	Lavenlair Farm	437 Deweys Bridge Rd.	(973) 820-3264
2.	Skenesborough Waterfront Community Park	Skenesborough Dr.	(518) 499-4071
3.	Skenesborough Museum	Skenesborough Dr.	(518) 499-0716
4.	Skene Manor	8 Potter Terr.	(518) 499-1906

TRAIL & TRAVEL NOTES

Birthplace of the U.S. Navy — Captured by American forces in 1774, the village of Skenesborough played a crucial role in the American Revolutionary War. The first fleet of American ships was built here to face the British stationed at Valcour Island further north on Lake Champlain. The following year, John Burgoyne marched his troops through this area en route to the Battles of Saratoga. After the Revolutionary War, Skenesborough was renamed Whitehall. With the completion of the Champlain Canal and the construction of the railroad, the village became a transportation and industrial hub, with the local silk industry growing in prominence.

Gothic Beauty — Perched high atop a hill over the Hudson River, Skene Manor is a historic home turned museum overlooking the town of Whitehall. Built by New York State Supreme Court Judge Joseph H. Potter in 1874, the Victorian-Gothic style mansion features 10 bedrooms, eight fireplaces, five chimneys, and three dining rooms. The main foyer has an original three-foot wall mural depicting a medieval hunt scene, and stained glass windows colorfully light several areas in the home. Owned and managed by a historic preservation group, tours of the mansion are seasonally available.

VISITOR INFORMATION

Washington County
(888) 203-8622
washingtoncounty.fun

AMENITIES

Whitehall

On the waterfront in Whitehall

Shops in Whitehall

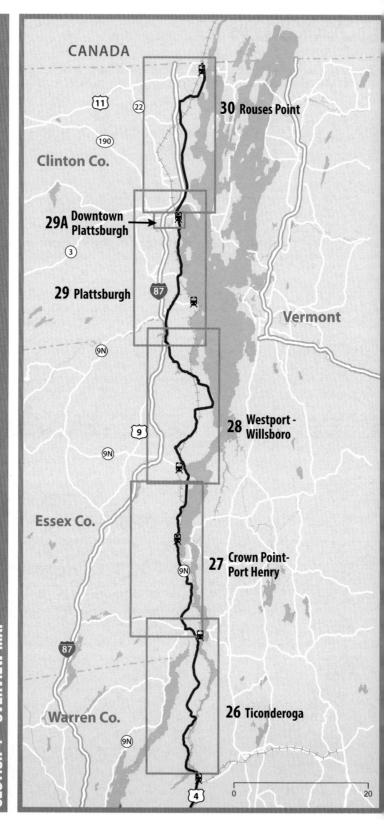

CANADA

(11) (22)

30 Rouses Point

(190)

Clinton Co.

(3)

29A Downtown Plattsburgh

29 Plattsburgh

87

Vermont

(9N)

(9)

28 Westport - Willsboro

(9N)

Essex Co.

27 Crown Point - Port Henry

(9N)

87

Warren Co.

26 Ticonderoga

(9N)

0   20

(4)

SECTION 4

WHITEHALL TO ROUSES POINT

The northern half of the Champlain Valley Trail, from Whitehall to the Canada border at Rouses Point, is an on-road bicycling route. This stretch of the Empire State Trail travels 123 miles over state highways, and is appropriate only for experienced cyclists comfortable sharing the road with swift traffic and navigating significant elevation changes. Bicyclists are rewarded with scenic views of Lake Champlain and its diverse shoreline. The route passes through the foothills of the Adirondack Mountains, extensive forests, rural landscapes, and historic villages and hamlets.

From Whitehall to Ticonderoga, the on-road route follows NYS Route 22, crossing the South Bay of Lake Champlain and winding through forested valleys and foothills of the Adirondack Mountains. This stretch typically has wide shoulders for bicyclists. Traffic here is generally light but fast-moving at 55mph, and there are some hilly sections. Riders should exercise caution between Ticonderoga and Westport—some stretches have thin margins of shoulder and limited site distances.

Ballard Park, off of Main Street in Westport, offers a bicycle kiosk with a maintenance rack, air pump, and map of the Empire State Trail. Between Westport and Keeseville, traffic is fairly limited, with lower speed limits in the villages, and much of the route is in view of Lake Champlain and the Green Mountains in Vermont.

From Keeseville to Plattsburgh, the route features rolling terrain, still along state highways. A 2-mile off-road paved trail, the Terry Gordon Bike Path, runs just south of Plattsburgh. The route through downtown Plattsburgh runs along lower-speed city streets. From Plattsburgh to the Canada border, traffic is fairly low but still swift-moving, and the route is relatively flat with sections of straight roads. For those who are up to the challenge, the region offers gorgeous scenery, impressive mountain views, quiet wilderness, and charming Adirondack communities.

THE ADIRONDACK PARK

The Adirondack Park, established in 1892 as one of the first "Forever Wild" Forest Preserves in the country, is the largest publicly protected area in the contiguous United States, spanning six million acres. The park, considered a great experiment in mixed-use conservation, preserves some of the land as permanent wilderness, while allowing residential and commercial occupancy throughout. The Adirondack Park contains an impressive 3,000 lakes and ponds and 30,000 miles of rivers and streams. The park is home to 46 "High Peaks," each soaring more than 4,000 feet in elevation.

HISTORY OF THE ADIRONDACKS

The Adirondack mountains were formed around 20 million years ago from fluctuations in the Earth's crust, and, incredibly, are still growing— the range has risen approximately one foot per century in recent history. Over one million years ago, when the changing climate led to the advance and retreat of massive ice sheets in the northern hemisphere, known as the Ice Age, glaciers sculpted the Adirondacks into the shapes we see today.

Artifacts discovered in the southern Adirondacks date back more than 10,000 years. Archeological evidence suggests that the first inhabitants of the region used the mountainous areas as seasonal hunting grounds, and primarily lived closer to lakes and river valleys, where it was easier to farm and trade. In the past 4,000 years, Mohawk, Mahican, Abenaki, Oneida, and other Native peoples have all considered the Adirondacks home territory. According to Tuscarora and Haudenosaunee historian Rick Hill, the Adirondack region was a primarily neutral territory shared by the Iroquois Confederacy with their allies in peacetime, though conflicts did arise between groups. The arrival of European settlers complicated the relationship of the Indigenous peoples to their land, and ultimately devastated their communities through disease, dishonest dealings, and open warfare. Many of those who survived colonization retreated from their homelands to Western New York and Canada.

The Six Nations Iroquois Cultural Center in Franklin County is a great resource for those interested in the cultural history of the Adirondacks, as is the Adirondack Experience in Blue Mountain Lake.

TOURISM IN THE ADIRONDACKS

Adventurous visitors can find endless reasons to head to the Adirondack Park—hiking, canoeing, bicycle touring, mountain biking, skiing, kayaking, rock climbing, boating, ice skating, birdwatching; nearly every outdoor activity is possible here. The Adirondacks are a famously popular vacation destination, particularly in the summer and fall, and welcome up to 12 million visitors annually. Foliage season is breathtakingly beautiful, when a rainbow of colors explodes across the mountains.

GETTING TO THE ADIRONDACKS

The vast Adirondack Park is accessible through many routes and modes of transportation. The Empire State Trail follows along what is known as 'The Adirondack Coast' of Lake Champlain, and is easily reachable by car via Interstate 87 (also known as the Adirondack Northway), and by Amtrak's Adirondack route. Bus services and flights to and from Plattsburgh International Airport are available but limited.

CAMPING AND ACCOMMODATIONS

The Adirondack region is a popular destination for summer vacations and for foliage viewing in the fall. While there are numerous campsites and other lodging opportunities in and around the park, they are often booked months in advance.

Adirondack bike racks in Downtown Plattsburgh

COMMUNITIES ALONG ROUTE

Essex County	Ticonderoga, Crown Point, Port Henry, Westport, Essex, Willsboro, Keeseville
Clinton County	Peru, Plattsburgh, Chazy, Champlain, Rouses Point

VISITOR INFORMATION

Essex County	co.essex.ny.us	(518) 873-3350
Clinton County	clintoncountygov.com	(518) 565-4700
Washington County	washingtoncounty.fun	(888) 203-8622

SAFETY & SECURITY

Universal Emergency Number: 911

Law Enforcement

State Police Troop G	Albany, Rensselaer, Saratoga & Washington Counties	(518) 783-3211
State Police Troop B	Essex and Clinton Counties	(518) 897-2000
Essex County Sheriff	Lewis	(518) 873-6321
Clinton County Sheriff	Plattsburgh	(518) 565-4300
Washington County Sheriff	Fort Edward	(518) 746-2522

Lake Champlain offers many scenic vistas

TRANSPORTATION

Amtrak Rail Stations (800-USA-RAIL)   amtrak.com
Whitehall (WHL)   154 Main St.
Ticonderoga (FTC)   NYS Rte. 74 & Sandy Redoubt
Port Henry (POH)   20 Park Pl.
Westport (WSP)   6705 Main St.
Port Kent (PRK)   Rte. 373 & Lake St.
Plattsburgh (PLB)   121 Bridge St.
Rouses Point (RSP)   68 Pratt St.

Urban & Regional Transit

Clinton County Public Transit	Multiple routes clintoncountypublictransit.com	(518) 561-1452
North Country Express	Plattsburgh to Potsdam northcountryexpress.net	(518) 563-3672
Essex County Public Transportation	Ticonderoga to Willsboro co.essex.ny.us	(800) 914-9266

Commercial Airports

| Plattsburgh International Airport (PBG) | flyplattsburgh.com | (518) 565-4795 |

HOSPITALS

| Champlain Valley Physicians Hospital Medical Center-Plattsburgh | (518) 585-3700 |
| Elizabethtown Community Hospital/ER-Ticonderoga | (518) 585-2831 |

Trail kiosk in Plattsburgh

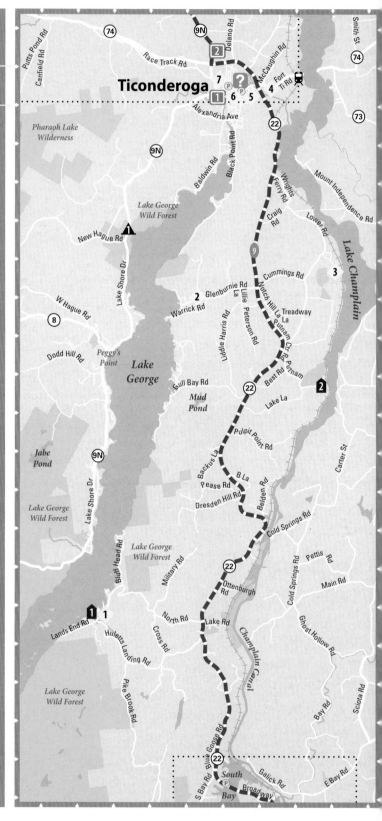

MAP 26   TICONDEROGA

1 MILE

Putts Pond Rd

Canfield Rd

74

Race Track Rd

Delano Rd

9N

2

McCaughin Rd

Fort
Ti Rd

Smith St

74

Ticonderoga

7

P

6   P

5

4

1

73

Alexandria Ave

22

Pharaoh Lake
Wilderness

Baldwin Rd

Black Point Rd

9N

Wrights
Ferry Rd

Mount Independence Rd

Lake George
Wild Forest

Craig
Rd

Lower Rd

New Hague Rd

Lake Shore Dr

9

Cummings Rd

3

Lake Champlain

Treadway

W Hague Rd

8

Glenburnie Rd

2

Warrick Rd

Lillie
Peterson Rd

Notch Hill La

Putnam

Dodd Hill Rd

Peggy's
Point

**Lake
George**

Liddle Harris Rd

Cr Rd

Putnam

Jabe
Pond

9N

Gull Bay Rd

Mud
Pond

Best Rd

Lake La

22

2

Carter St

Pulpit Point Rd

Lake Shore Dr

Backus La

B La

Belden Rd

Cold Springs Rd

Cold Springs Rd

Pettis
Rd

Lake George
Wild Forest

Pease Rd

Dresden Hill Rd

Main Rd

22

Ottenburgh
Rd

Champlain Canal

Ghost Hollow Rd

Bluff Head Rd

Military Rd

North Rd

Lake Rd

1

1

Lands End Rd

Huletts Landing Rd

Cross
Rd

Pike Brook Rd

Lake George
Wild Forest

Blue Goose Rd

S Bay Rd

22

South
Bay

P

Broadway

Galick Rd

E Bay Rd

Scioto Rd

Bay Rd

THINGS TO SEE & DO

1.	Huletts Park	6303 Sunset Bay Rd.	(518) 746-2451
	Friends of Historical Huletts	2010 Lands End Rd.	
2.	Anthony's Nose Preserve	181-259 Schwerdfeger Rd.	(518) 644-9673
3.	Billy Bob's Orchard	720 County Rte. 2	(518) 222-5171
4.	Fort Ticonderoga	102 Fort Ti Rd.	(518) 585-2821
5.	Ticonderoga Heritage Museum	137 Montcalm St.	(518) 585-2696
	LaChute River Walk Trail at Bicentennial Park		
6.	Star Trek Original Series Set Tour	112 Montcalm St.	(518) 503-5497
7.	Ticonderoga Historical Society	6 Moses Cir.	(518) 585-7868

TRAIL & TRAVEL NOTES

Fort Ticonderoga — The name "Ticonderoga" originates from the Iroquois word 'tekontaró:ken,' meaning "it is at the junction of two waterways." Indigenous peoples used the area to portage their watercraft for centuries prior to European contact. With its strategic location at the southern end of Lake Champlain and the northern tip of Lake George, Fort Ticonderoga played a significant role in the American Revolutionary War. The star-shaped fort was built by the French during the Colonial period, later taken over by the British, and then famously captured by Ethan Allen and Benedict Arnold for the colonists in 1775. Today, visitors to Fort Ticonderoga can tour exhibits on colonial life and military history, attend battle re-enactments, and participate in many seasonal activities and events.

Pencil and Paper — Local deposits of pure graphite ore around Ticonderoga, found on Lead Hill in 1815, uniquely positioned the area for the production of pencils. The Ticonderoga Pencil was first patented in 1839, and while the name remains in use, pencil manufacturing has since dispersed around the country. Paper mills, however, which developed in Ticonderoga in the nineteenth century, have persisted and remain a large industry in the town today.

"Boldly go where no man has gone before." — Star Trek fans will find hidden treasure in Ticonderoga—a re-created set of the 1960s television series is lovingly preserved here! The owners of the set host an annual Star Trek festival, which typically features at least one original cast member as a speaker.

VISITOR INFORMATION

Ticonderoga Heritage Museum & Visitors Center
137 Montcalm Street
(518) 585-2696
ticonderogany.com

AMENITIES

Ticonderoga

On-road views in northern Warren County

MAP 27   CROWN POINT - PORT HENRY

1 MILE

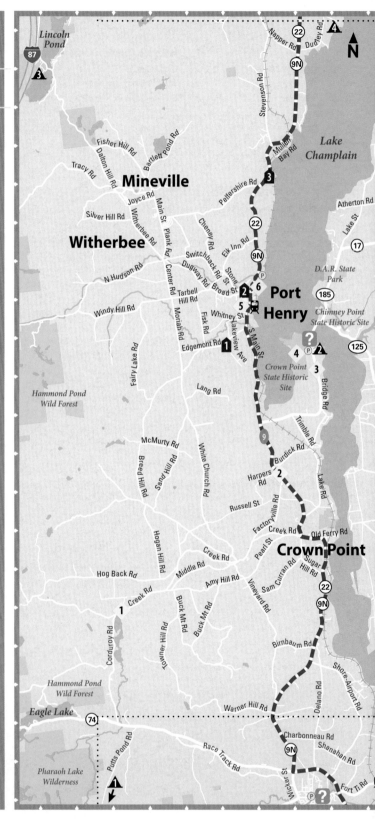

Lincoln Pond

87 3

Fisher Hill Rd
Bartlett Pond Rd
Tracy Rd
Dalton Hill Rd

Mineville

Joyce Rd
Silver Hill Rd
Witherbee Rd
Main St
Plank Rd

Witherbee

N Hudson Rd
Center Rd
Windy Hill Rd

Pelfershire Rd

Cheney Rd
Elk Inn Rd
Switchback Rd
Stone St
Dugway Rd
Broad St

22
9N

P

2 6

Port Henry

Tarbell Hill Rd
Moriah Rd
Fisk Rd
Whitney St
Lakeview Ave
S Main St

5

1

Edgemont Rd

Napper Rd
Dudley Rd
22
4

9N

Stevenson Rd

Mullan Bay Rd

3

Lake Champlain

Atherton Rd
Lake St
17

D.A.R. State Park

185

Chimney Point State Historic Site

?
P
4 2
125

Crown Point State Historic Site

3
Bridge Rd

Fairy Lake Rd

Hammond Pond Wild Forest

Lang Rd

McMurty Rd
White Church Rd
Breed Hill Rd
Sand Hill Rd

9

Burdick Rd

2

Harpers Rd
Russell St

Trimble Rd
Lake Rd

Factorville Rd
Creek Rd
Pearl St

Old Ferry Rd
Sugar Hill Rd

Crown Point

Hogan Hill Rd
Middle Rd
Creek Rd
Amy Hill Rd
Sam Curran Rd
Vineyard Rd

22
9N

Hog Back Rd
Creek Rd
Buck Mt Rd

1

Corduroy Rd
Towner Hill Rd

Birnbaum Rd

Delano Rd
Shore-Airport Rd

Hammond Pond Wild Forest

Eagle Lake 74

Warner Hill Rd

Charbonneau Rd
9N
Shanahan Rd

Pharaoh Lake Wilderness

Putts Pond Rd
Race Track Rd

Wicker St
P
?
Fort Tr Rd

1

N

THINGS TO SEE & DO

1.	Penfield Homestead Museum	703 Creek Rd.	(518) 597-3804
2.	Gunnison Lakeshore Orchards	3208 NYS Rte. 9N	(518) 597-9222
3.	Champlain Memorial Lighthouse	Bridge Rd.	
4.	Crown Point State Historic Site	21 Grandview Dr.	(518) 597-4666
5.	Iron Center Museum	34 Park Pl.	(518) 546-3587
6.	Port Henry Beach	Beach Rd.	(518) 546-7123

TRAIL & TRAVEL NOTES

His Majesty's Fort of Crown Point — Mysterious stone ruins beside stunning views of Lake Champlain, the Crown Point Bridge, and the Adirondack Mountains greet visitors to Crown Point State Historic Site. Much like Fort Ticonderoga, the fortifications here were built by the French, repossessed by the British, and captured by the Americans. The historic park offers tours and a museum which includes multimedia programs, large scale models, and an exhibit of original artifacts recovered from the site by archaeologists.

Champlain Lighthouse — The Champlain Memorial Lighthouse commemorates Samuel de Champlain, the first European to navigate the lake in 1609. The lighthouse, opened in 1858, is decorated with bronze sculptures by Carl Augustus Heber and Auguste Rodin. Nearby state campsites are within walking distance to the lighthouse.

American Loch Ness Monster — An apocryphal quote by Samuel de Champlain, on his inaugural visit to the lake, cites "a 20-foot serpent thick as a barrel, and a head like a horse." Whether this is true or not, people have been reporting the existence of a freshwater serpent of fantastic proportions in Lake Champlain ever since. Fondly known as "Champy" or "Champ" in communities all around the lake, Port Henry claims to be the home of this local celebrity.

VISITOR INFORMATION

Lake Champlain Visitors Center
814 Bridge Rd.
(518) 597-4649
lakechamplainregion.com

AMENITIES

Port Henry

Lake Champlain Bridge

Crown Point State Park

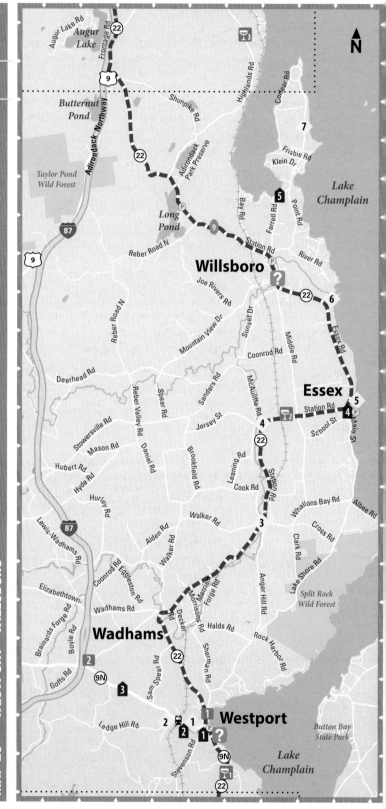

THINGS TO SEE & DO

1.	Essex County Fairgrounds	Main St.	(518) 962-8650
2.	Depot Theatre	6705 Main St.	(518) 962-4449
3.	Whallonsburg Grange Hall	1610 NYS Rte. 22	(518) 963-7777
4.	Boquet Octagonal Schoolhouse	2214 NYS Rte. 22	
5.	Lake Champlain Ferry to Charlotte, VT	1 Main St.	(802) 864-9804
6.	Noblewood Park & Beach	96 Noblewood Pk.	(518) 963-8933
7.	Adsit Log Cabin	852 Point Rd.	(518) 963-4897

TRAIL & TRAVEL NOTES

Vacation Town — Westport, the birthplace of the iconic Adirondack chair, rose to prominence as an upscale resort haven for out-of-towners in the nineteenth century. As modes of transportation expanded and trips to farther destinations became feasible for East Coast travelers, the Adirondacks briefly fell out of style. However, since the 1950s, Westport has slowly regained its popularity as a vacation destination. Gorgeous views of Lake Champlain and the Green Mountains are visible all along the route here.

"Door of the Country" — For many centuries prior to colonization, Lake Champlain acted as a border between the Indigenous lands of the Mohawk and Abenaki. To the Mohawk who lived on the New York side, one of the names for the lake was 'Kaniá:tare tsi kahnhokà:ronte,' meaning "door of the country" or "doorway lake." The Mohawk were farmers who grew corn, beans, and squash, supplementing this diet by hunting, fishing, and trapping in the Adirondacks and along Lake Champlain. Many of the Mohawk and Abenaki peoples who survived the dispossession of their ancestral lands fled to Canada.

VISITOR INFORMATION

Lake Champlain Visitors Center
(518) 597-4649
lakechamplainregion.com

AMENITIES

Westport	
Willboro	

Adsit Log Cabin

Gorgeous vistas of Lake Champlain

I MILE

MAP 29 PLATTSBURGH

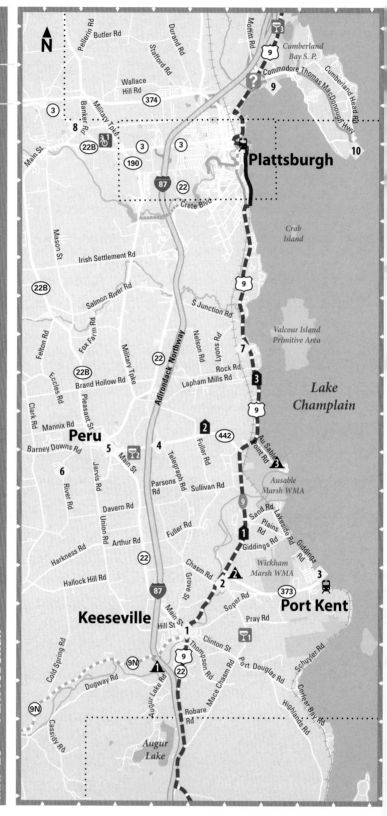

N

Pellerin Rd
Butler Rd
Durand Rd
Moffitt Rd
9
Cumberland Bay S. P.
Commodore Thomas MacDonough Hwy
Cumberland Head Rd
Stafford Rd
Wallace Hill Rd
374
9
3
Military Tpke
Banker Rd
Main St
8
22B
3
3
190
87
22
Crete Blvd
Plattsburgh
10
Crab Island
Mason St
Irish Settlement Rd
22B
S Junction Rd
Valcour Island Primitive Area
Salmon River Rd
Fox Farm Rd
Felton Rd
Military Tpke
22
Nelson Rd
Lyons Rd
Rock Rd
9
7
3
9
Lake Champlain
Eccles Rd
22B
Brand Hollow Rd
Pleasant St
Clark Rd
Mannix Rd
Lapham Mills Rd
Peru
2
442
Au Sable Point Rd
3
Barney Downs Rd
5
2
4
Fuller Rd
Ausable Marsh WMA
6
River Rd
Jarvis Rd
Main St
Telegraph Rd
Sullivan Rd
9
Sand Rd
Plains Rd
Lakeside Rd
Giddings Rd
Parsons Rd
Davern Rd
Union Rd
Arthur Rd
Fuller Rd
1
Giddings Rd
Wickham Marsh WMA
Harkness Rd
22
Chasm Rd
Grove St
2
2
3
Hallock Hill Rd
Soper Rd
373
Port Kent
87
Keeseville
Main St
Hill St
1
Clinton St
Pray Rd
1
9N
9
9N
Cold Spring Rd
Dugway Rd
Augur Lake Rd
22
Thompson Rd
Robare Rd
Mace Chasm Rd
Port Douglas Rd
Schuyler Rd
Cassidy Rd
Augur Lake
Highlands Rd
Corlear Bay Rd

THINGS TO SEE & DO

#			
1.	Adirondack Architectural Heritage	1745 Main St.	(716) 694-7406
	Anderson Falls Heritage Museum	96 Clinton St.	(716) 694-7406
2.	Ausable Chasm	2144 US Rte. 9	(716) 692-2413
	North Star Underground Railroad Museum	1131 Mace Chasm Rd.	(518) 834-5180
3.	Lake Champlain Ferry to Burlington, VT	1 NYS Rte. 313	(716) 213-0554
	Port Kent Beach	1 NYS Rte. 373	
4.	Rulfs Orchard	531 Bear Swamp Rd.	(518) 643-8636
5.	Heyworth Mason Park	2948-2956 Mason Hill Rd.	(716) 693-1885
6.	Babbie Rural & Farm Learning Museum	250 River Rd.	(716) 434-5665
7.	Stone Ledge Sculpture Garden	3901 US Rte. 9	
8.	Banker Orchards	1037 NYS Rte. 3	(716) 694-4400
9.	Cumberland Bay State Park	152 Cumberland Head Rd.	(716) 743-1614
	Plattsburgh City Beach	4 Beach Rd.	(518) 563-7642
10.	Lake Champlain Ferry to Grand Isle, VT	820 C.T. McDonough Hwy	(716) 689-1440

TRAIL & TRAVEL NOTES

Ausable Chasm — Breathtaking views of Ausable Chasm can be seen from the Ausable Chasm Bridge, which the Empire State Trail route crosses north of Keeseville. The Ausable Gorge was carved out of 500-million-year-old Potsdam sandstone by the Ausable River and the movement and melting of glaciers after the last ice age. The sandstone has preserved many fossils, some of which are on display at the New York State Museum in Albany. Today, Ausable Chasm is privately owned and offers lantern tours, whitewater rafting, rappelling, hiking, mountain biking, rock climbing, tubing, and caving.

Follow the North Star — The route north charts the way of numerous formerly enslaved people who followed the North Star towards freedom. The North Country Underground Railroad Historical Association preserves and interprets the history of the Underground Railroad, slavery, and abolition along the Upper Hudson River. The North Star Underground Railroad Museum, a testament to human rights, exhibits the personal stories and harrowing escapes of the time period.

VISITOR INFORMATION

Adirondack Coast Visitors Bureau
7061 US Rte. 9
(518) 563-1000
goadirondack.com

AMENITIES

Keeseville R_x

Ausable Chasm

1 MILE

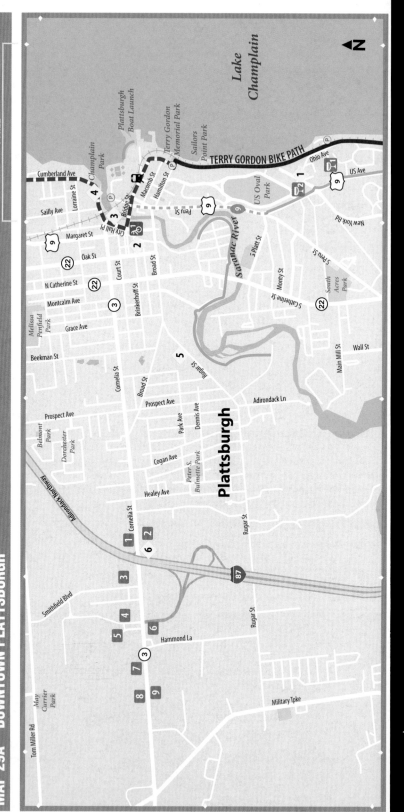

N

Lake Champlain

Plattsburgh Boat Launch

Terry Gordon Memorial Park

Sailors Point Park

TERRY GORDON BIKE PATH

Ohio Ave

US Ave

Cumberland Ave

Champlain Park

Lorraine St

Sailly Ave

Bridge St

City Hall Pl

Macomb St

Hamilton St

Peru St

US Oval Park

New York Rd

Margaret St

Oak St

Court St

Broad St

S Plat St

Monty St

S Peru St

N Catherine St

Montcalm Ave

Brinkerhoff St

S Catherine St

South Acres Park

Melissa Penfield Park

Grace Ave

Beekman St

Cornelia St

Broad St

Rugar St

Saranac River

Main Mill St

Wall St

Prospect Ave

Prospect Ave

Park Ave

Dennis Ave

Adirondack Ln

Belmont Park

Dorchester Park

Cogan Ave

Peter S. Bulmette Park

Plattsburgh

Healey Ave

Rugar St

Adirondack Northway

Cornelia St

Smithfield Blvd

Hammond La

Rugar St

May Currier Park

Military Tpke

Tom Miller Rd

87

THINGS TO SEE & DO

1.	War of 1812 Museum	31 Washington Rd.	(518) 566-1814
	Clinton County Historical Association and Museum	310 Fourth St.	(877) 873-6322
	Kids' Station Children's Museum	454 Main St.	(716) 284-2800
	Plattsburgh Air Force Base Museum	825 Depot Ave. W	(716) 300-8477
2.	The Strand Center for the Arts	9990 Porter Rd.	(716) 297-1323
3.	Macdonough Monument	701 Whirlpool St.	(716) 285-3575
4.	Kent-Delord House Museum	425 Third St.	(518) 561-1035
5.	Plattsburgh State Art Museum	5777 Lewiston Rd.	(716) 286-6661
6.	Champy's Fun City	411 NYS Rte. 3	

Eclectic downtown Plattsburgh

TRAIL & TRAVEL NOTES

Battle of Plattsburgh — Visitors to Plattsburgh in September may find themselves startled by cannon fire, people in eighteenth century apparel, and the sound of bagpipes. The Battle of Plattsburgh, which decisively ended British occupation of the region in the Battle of 1812, is commemorated each year with a festival downtown. The Kent-Delord Museum, open seasonally, hosts artifacts and exhibits on the Battle.

Arts and Culture — Several thousand college students call Plattsburgh home during the academic year, and they can often be found in the charming downtown's cafes, bars, and eclectic shops. The downtown culture is fun and artsy, with many unique murals and outdoor sculptures.

Museums and Military Bases — Plattsburgh served as a strategic military location for over 400 years, from the first forts of European colonists to the former Plattsburgh Air Force Base. A cluster of museums located in some of the former base's historic barrack buildings showcase Plattsburgh's extensive military history.

VISITOR INFORMATION

Adirondack Coast Visitors Bureau
(518) 563-1000
goadirondack.com

AMENITIES

Plattsburgh   🛈 🍴 ✏ 🛍 🚻 Rx

Young re-enacters at the Battle of Plattsburgh festival

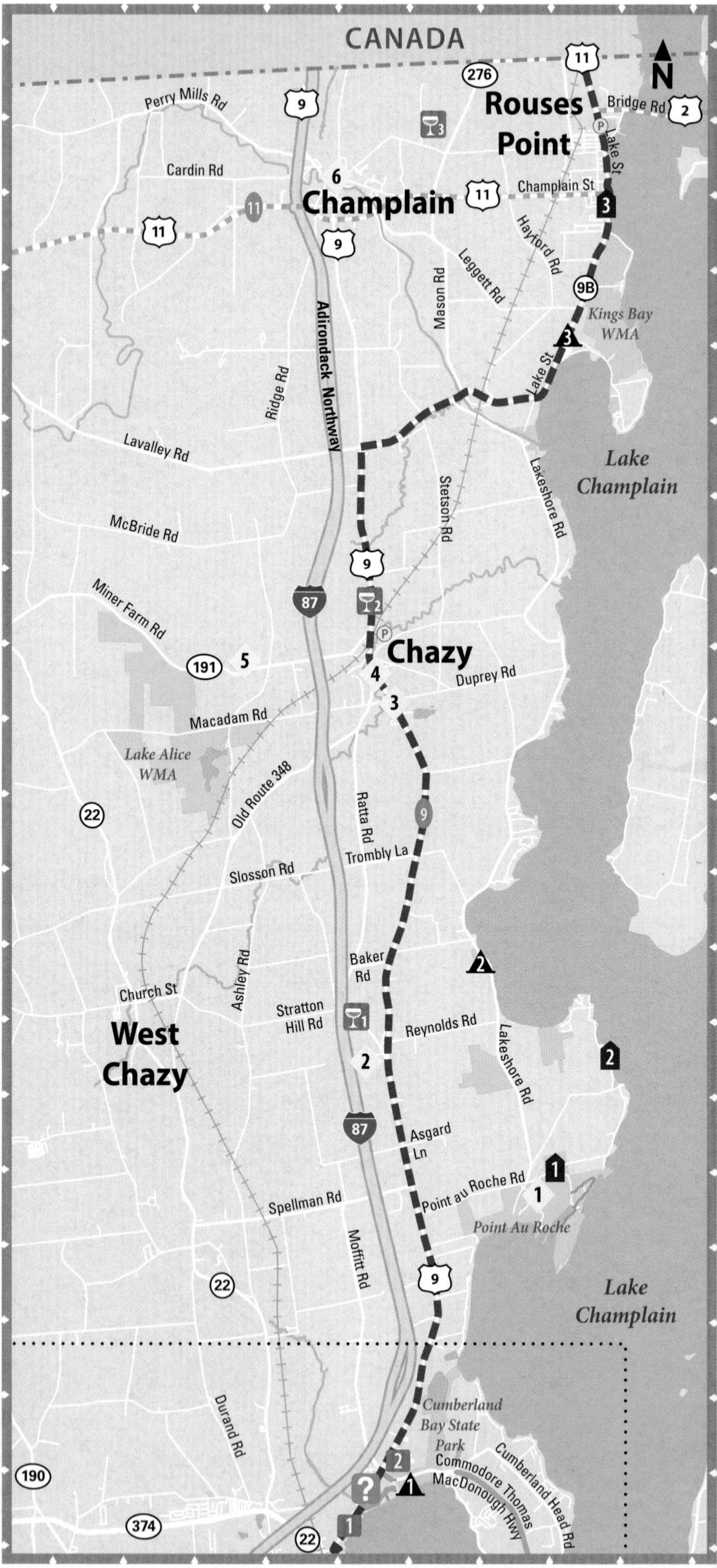

1 MILE

MAP 30   ROUSES POINT

CANADA

Perry Mills Rd

276

Rouses
Point

Bridge Rd

2

11

9

N

Cardin Rd

6

Champlain

11

Champlain St

Lake St

3

11

Hayford Rd

9B

Leggett Rd

3

Kings Bay
WMA

Mason Rd

Lake St

Ridge Rd

Lavalley Rd

Lakeshore Rd

Lake
Champlain

McBride Rd

Adirondack Northway

Stetson Rd

Miner Farm Rd

9

191

5

87

Macadam Rd

2

Chazy

Lake Alice
WMA

Old Route 348

4

Duprey Rd

22

3

Slosson Rd

Ratta Rd

Trombly La

9

Ashley Rd

Church St

Baker
Rd

2

2

West
Chazy

Stratton
Hill Rd

1

Reynolds Rd

Lakeshore Rd

2

87

2

Asgard
Ln

1

Spellman Rd

Moffitt Rd

Point au Roche Rd

1

Point Au Roche

22

9

Durand Rd

Lake
Champlain

190

Cumberland
Bay State
Park

374

22

2

?

1

Commodore Thomas
MacDonough Hwy

Cumberland
Head Rd

THINGS TO SEE & DO

1.	Point Au Roche State Park	19 Camp Red Cloud Rd.	(518) 563-0369
2.	Bechard's Sugar House	61 Sanger Ln.	(518) 846-7498
3.	Chazy Orchards	9486 US Rte. 9	(518) 846-7171
4.	Alice T. Miner Museum	9618 US Rte. 9	(518) 846-7336
5.	William H. Miner Agricultural Research Institute	1034 Miner Farm Rd.	(518) 846-7121
6.	Samuel De Champlain History Center	202 Elm St.	(518) 298-1609

TRAIL & TRAVEL NOTES

Biosphere — The Champlain-Adirondack Biosphere Network was established by UNESCO in 1989 to preserve and protect the unique web of ecosystems surrounding Lake Champlain. The biosphere comprises over seven million acres, including extensive forests, rivers, wetlands, and other lakes in addition to Lake Champlain. The reserve is one of the largest and the most populous in the U.S., inhabited by more than 300,000 people and within a day's drive of 60 million people living in the U.S. and Canada. A popular destination for birdwatchers, more than 300 species of birds breed, overwinter, or pass through the Lake Champlain Basin during migration.

Fruitful Endeavors — Clinton County is home to an array of wineries, maple sugar houses, and orchards, many of which are conveniently located alongside the Empire State Trail route. Stop by for a wine tasting, a piece of maple candy, or a cider donut.

Connections to Canada — The Empire State Trail ends at the Canada border, but your trip doesn't need to end there! Just across the border, the route continues as part of Le Route Verte, a network of over 5,000 km (that's over 3,100 miles) of bicycle routes across Québec. Montreal itself has over 400 miles of bikeways, and is just over 50 miles north of the border. For more information on crossing the border, see page 135.

VISITOR INFORMATION

Adirondack Coast Visitors Bureau
(518) 563-1000
goadirondack.com

AMENITIES

Chazy		
Rouses Point		R_x

Riding through the Champlain Valley

Sailboats at Rouses Point

LODGING

New York City (Maps 1 - 3) offers such a dense concentration of options for lodging accommodations that it would be impossible to list them all. Visit nycgo.com or use a commercial online travel site for more resources for planning a trip to New York City. The lists below are meant to be helpful suggestions for options close to the trail; they are not exhaustive and are subject to change.

MAP 4 — BRONX - YONKERS

Hotels / Motels

1	Edge Hotel	514 W 168th St.	(212) 543-0005
2	Rodeway Inn Bronx Zoo	3070-72 Webster Ave.	(718) 654-5500
3	Yonkers Gateway Motel	300 Yonkers Ave.	(914) 476-6600
4	Hyatt Place New York/Yonkers	7000 Mall Walk	(914) 377-1400
5	Royal Regency Hotel Yonkers	165 Tuckahoe Rd.	(914) 476-6200
6	Hampton Inn Yonkers	160 Corporate Blvd.	(914) 377-1144
7	Residence Inn Yonkers	7 Executive Blvd.	(914) 476-4600
	Courtyard Yonkers	5 Executive Blvd.	(914) 476-2400
8	Hampton Inn Westchester	559 Tuckahoe Rd.	(914) 963-3200

MAP 5 — ARDSLEY - PLEASANTVILLE

Hotels / Motels

1	Hilton Garden Inn Dobbs Ferry	201 Ogden Ave.	(914) 591-4300
2	Ardsley Acres Hotel Court	560 Saw Mill River Rd.	(914) 693-2700
3	Tarrytown House Estate	49 E Sunnyside Ln.	(914) 591-8200
4	Hampton Inn White Plains/Tarrytown	200 W Main St.	(914) 592-5680
5	Westchester Marriott	670 White Plains Rd.	(914) 631-2200
6	Sheraton Tarrytown Hotel	600 White Plains Rd.	(914) 332-7900
7	SpringHill Suites Tarrytown	480 White Plains Rd.	(914) 366-4600
8	Courtyard Tarrytown	475 White Plains Rd.	(914) 631-1122
9	Castle Hotel & Spa	400 Benedict Ave.	(914) 631-1980
10	La Quinta Inn White Plains-Elmsford	540 Saw Mill River Rd.	(914) 592-3300
11	Comfort Inn & Suites	20 Saw Mill River Rd.	(914) 592-8600

MAP 6 — BRIARCLIFF MANOR - YORKTOWN HEIGHTS

B&Bs / Inns

1	Crabtree's Kittle House	11 Kittle Rd.	(914) 666-8044

MAP 8 — BREWSTER

Hotels / Motels

1	Comfort Inn	7-11 Peach Lake Rd.	(845) 221-1941
2	Heidi's Inn	1270 NY 22	(845) 279-8011
3	Bel Air Motor Lodge	1574 NY 22	(845) 279-3350

MAP 9 — HOPEWELL JUNCTION

B&Bs / Inns

1	Station Inn Pawling	7 Memorial Ave.	(845) 266-6262
2	Bykenhulle House B&B	21 Bykenhulle Rd.	(845) 242-3260
3	Curry Estate	2737 NY 52	(845) 221-1941
4	Inn at Arbor Ridge	17 NY 376	(845) 227-7700

MAP 10 — POUGHKEEPSIE

Hotels / Motels

1	Best Western Plus - The Falls	50 Red Oaks Mill Rd.	(845) 462-5770
2	Holiday Inn Express Poughkeepsie	2750 South Rd.	(845) 473-1151
3	Quality Inn Poughkeepsie	536 W Haight Ave.	(845) 454-1010

MAP 10A — DOWNTOWN POUGHKEEPSIE
Hotels / Motels
| 1 | Poughkeepsie Grand Hotel | 40 Civic Center Plz. | (845) 485-5300 |

MAP 11 — HIGHLAND - NEW PALTZ
Hotels / Motels
1	Atlas Motor Lodge	125 Tillson Ave Ext.	(845) 691-8300
2	Surestay Plus Highland Poughkeepsie	3423 US 9W	(845) 834-2584
3	Rodeway Inn New Paltz	601 Main St.	(845) 883-7373

B&Bs / Inns
1	Inn at Twaalfskill	144 Vineyard Ave.	(845) 691-3605
2	Fox Hill B&B	55 S Chodikee Lake Rd.	(845) 691-8151
3	Black Creek B&B	430 N Riverside Rd.	(914) 494-2154
4	Gatehouse Gardens	5 Gatehouse Rd.	(845) 255-8817
5	The Inn at Kettleboro	321 NY 208	(914) 213-2487

MAP 11A — DOWNTOWN NEW PALTZ
Hotels / Motels
| 1 | Americas Best Value Inn New Paltz | 7 Terwilliger Ln. | (845) 255-8865 |
| 2 | Hampton Inn New Paltz | 4 S Putt Corners Rd. | (845) 255-4200 |

B&Bs / Inns / Hostels
| 1 | New Paltz Hostel | 145 Main St. | (845) 255-6676 |
| 2 | Moondance Ridge B&B | 55 Shivertown Rd. | (845) 255-4161 |

MAP 12 — ROSENDALE
B&Bs / Inns
| 1 | 1850 House Inn & Tavern | 435 Main St. | (845) 658-7800 |

MAP 12A — DOWNTOWN KINGSTON
Hotels / Motels
| 1 | Hotel Kinsley | 301 Wall St. | (845) 768-3620 |
| 2 | Best Western Plus | 503 Washington Ave. | (845) 338-0400 |

B&Bs / Inns
1	A Kingston B&B	131 Fair St.	(845) 514-2365
2	1910 House B&B	133 Green St.	(917) 757-9692
3	The Forsyth B&B	85 Abeel St.	(845) 481-9148

MAP 13 — KINGSTON
Hotels / Motels
1	Hampton Inn Kingston	1307 Ulster Ave.	(845) 382-2600
2	Residence Inn Kingston	800 Frank Sottile Blvd.	(845) 383-3695
	Courtyard Kingston	500 Frank Sottile Blvd.	(845) 382-2300
3	Rhinebeck Motel	6938 US 9	(845) 876-5900

B&Bs / Inns / Cabins
1	Hutton Brickyards	200 North St.	(845) 213-4742
2	The Baker House	65 West Market St.	(917) 680-1855
3	Chestnut Suite	11 Chestnut St.	(845) 876-6203
4	The Gables of Rhinebeck	6358 Mill St.	(631) 766-6871
	Beekman Arms & Delamater Inn	6387 Mill St.	(845) 876-7077
5	WhistleWood Farm	52 Pells Rd.	(845) 876-6838
6	Red Hook Country Inn	7460 S Broadway	(845) 758-8445
7	The Grand Dutchess	7571 Old Post Rd.	(845) 758-5818

MAP 14 — TIVOLI - GERMANTOWN

B&Bs / Inns

1	Hotel Tivoli	53 Broadway	(845) 757-2100
2	Suminski Innski	8 Friendship St.	(845) 757-5005
3	The Central House	220 Main St.	(518) 537-7722

MAP 15 — CATSKILL - HUDSON

B&Bs / Inns

1	Mount Merino Manor	4317 NY 23	(518) 828-5583

MAP 15A — DOWNTOWN HUDSON

Hotels / Motels

1	The Wick, Hudson	41 Cross St.	(518) 249-6825
2	St. Charles Hotel	16 Park Pl.	(518) 822-9900
3	Rivertown Lodge	731 Warren St.	(518) 512-0954

B&Bs / Inns

1	Wm. Farmer and Sons	20 S Front St.	(518) 828-1635
2	Hudson Mariner	26 Warren St.	(518) 254-8766
3	The Inn at 34	34 S Second St.	(888) 279-0365
4	Hudson B&B	136 Union St.	(518) 929-6199
5	The Howard Hotel	216 Warren St.	(518) 303-6650
6	Batterby House	251 Allen St.	(518) 822-9229
7	The Maker Hotel	302 Warren St.	(518) 509-2620
8	Hudson City B&B	326 Allen St.	(518) 822-8044
9	The Nest Hudson	330 Union St.	(518) 302-9400
10	The Nautical Nest	12 City Hall Pl.	(518) 302-9400
11	The Amelia Hotel	339 Allen St.	(518) 768-7900
12	The Hudson Milliner	415 Warren St.	(917) 930-4302
13	Westcott House B&B	24 N 5th St.	(518) 828-2803
14	The Hudson Whaler Hotel	542 Warren St.	(518) 217-4334

MAP 16 — HUDSON - KINDERHOOK

B&Bs / Inns

1	Micosta Leisure Inn	3007 County Rte. 20	(518) 451-0109
2	Mile Hill B&B	2461 County Rte. 21	(917) 691-8757

MAP 18 — EAST GREENBUSH - RENSSELAER

Hotels / Motels

1	Comfort Inn East Greenbush	99 Miller Rd.	(347) 382-9645
2	Castle Inn	1565 Columbia Tpke.	(518) 477-9906
3	Victorian Motel	752 Columbia Tpke.	(518) 477-6160
4	Fairfield Inn East Greenbush	124 Troy Rd.	(518) 477-7984
5	Hampton Inn East Greenbush	25 Hampton Inn Dr.	(518) 477-9700
6	Residence Inn East Greenbush	3 Tech Valley Dr.	(518) 720-3600
7	Holiday Inn Express East Greenbush	8 Empire Dr.	(518) 286-1011
8	Capital Inn & Suites	110 Columbia Tpke.	(518) 472-1360

MAP 18A — DOWNTOWN ALBANY

Hotels / Motels

1	Holiday Inn Express Albany	300 Broadway	(518) 434-4111
2	Fairfield Inn Albany	74 State St.	(518) 434-7410
3	Hilton Albany	40 Lodge St.	(518) 462-6611
4	Renaissance Albany Hotel	144 State St.	(518) 992-2500
5	Hampton Inn Albany	25 Chapel St.	(518) 432-7000
6	Hilton Garden Inn Albany	62 New Scotland Ave.	(518) 396-3500

B&Bs / Inns

1	State St Mansion	281 State St.	(518) 462-6780
2	The Morgan State House	393 State St.	(888) 427-6063
3	Washington Park Inn	634 Madison Ave.	(518) 930-4700
4	The Argus Hotel	8 Thurlow Terr.	(518) 930-4700

MAP 19 — ALBANY - TROY

Hotels / Motels

1	TownePlace Suites Albany	22 Holland Ave.	(518) 860-1500
2	Four Points Albany	3 Mount Hope Way	(518) 949-2220
3	Comfort Inn Glenmont	37 US 9W	(518) 362-1076

B&Bs / Inns

1	Gardner Farm Inn	59 Brunswick Rd.	(917) 509-5110

MAP 19A — DOWNTOWN TROY

Hotels / Motels

1	Franklin Square Inn Troy	1 4th St.	(518) 274-8800
2	Courtyard Troy Waterfront	515 River St.	(518) 240-1000

MAP 20 — COHOES - WATERFORD

Hotels / Motels

1	Hilton Garden Inn Troy	235 Hoosick St.	(518) 272-1700

B&Bs / Inns

1	Olde Judge Mansion	3300 6th Ave.	(518) 331-3945
2	Oakcliff B&B	78 Church Hill Rd.	(518) 281-4434

MAP 21 — MECHANICVILLE - STILLWATER

B&Bs / Inns

1	Maple Shade B&B	112 Wilbur Rd.	(518) 587-9235

MAP 22A — SCHUYLERVILLE - HUDSON CROSSING PARK

B&Bs / Inns / Cabins

1	Schuyler Yacht Basin	1 Ferry St.	(518) 695-3193
2	Old Saratoga Inn	177 Broad St.	(518) 695-9997
3	Dovegate Inn	184 Broad St.	(518) 695-3699

MAP 23 — FORT EDWARD - HUDSON FALLS

Hotels / Motels

1	Spring Motor Inn	215 Broadway	(518) 747-0778

MAP 23A — GLENS FALLS

Hotels / Motels

1	The Queensbury Hotel	88 Ridge St.	(518) 792-1121

B&Bs / Inns

1	The Glens Falls Inn	25 Sherman Ave.	(518) 409-4204
2	The Bell House Inn	153 Bay St.	(518) 745-0200

MAP 24 — FORT ANN

Hotels / Motels

1	From the Heart Motel	16 George St.	(518) 639-4411

MAP 25 — WHITEHALL

B&Bs / Inns

1	Chamberlin Farms	116 County Rte. 17A	(518) 769-2238

MAP 26 — TICONDEROGA

Hotels / Motels

1	Stone House Motel	9 Montcalm St.	(518) 585-7394
	Circle Court Motel	6 Montcalm St.	(518) 585-7660
2	Super 8 Ticonderoga	1144 Wicker St.	(518) 503-0591
	Best Western Plus Ticonderoga	260 Burgoyne Rd.	(518) 585-2378

B&Bs / Inns / Cabins

1	Huletts on Lake George	4100 Margot Ln.	(518) 499-1234
2	The Inn on Lake Champlain	428 County Rte. 3	(518) 547-8406

MAP 27 — CROWN POINT - PORT HENRY

B&Bs / Inns / Cabins

1	Edgemont Inn	284 Edgemont Rd.	(518) 546-4123
2	The Village Inn	1 Star Way	(518) 250-0993
3	Nelson's Cottages	5046 NY 9N	(518) 546-7361

MAP 28 — WESTPORT - WILLSBORO

Hotels / Motels

1	Westport Lakeside Motel	80 Champlain Ave.	(518) 962-4501
2	Hilltop Motel	35 Youngs Rd.	(518) 962-4401

B&Bs / Inns

1	The Inn in Westport	1234 Stevenson Rd.	(518) 335-1966
2	Westport Hotel and Tavern	6691 Main St.	(518) 962-4001
3	Dacy Meadow Farm	7078 NY 9N	(518) 962-8339
4	The Essex Inn on the Adirondack Coast	2297 Main St.	(518) 963-4400
5	Willsboro Inn	361 Farrell Rd.	(518) 418-5116

MAP 29 — PLATTSBURGH

B&Bs / Inns / Cabins

1	The Shamrock Inn	2445 US 9	(518) 834-9770
2	Iroquois Campground & RV Park	270 Bear Swamp Rd.	(518) 569-6972
3	Valcour Inn	3712 US 9	(518) 564-2038

MAP 29A — DOWNTOWN PLATTSBURGH

Hotels / Motels

1	Days Inn Plattsburgh	406 NY 3	(518) 561-5000
2	Comfort Inn Plattsburgh	411 NY 3	(518) 907-4562
3	Best Western Plus Plattsburgh	446 NY 3	(518) 561-7750
4	La Quinta Inn Plattsburgh	16 Plaza Blvd.	(518) 562-4000
5	America's Best Value Inn Plattsburgh	19 Booth Dr.	(518) 563-0222
6	Holiday Inn Express Plattsburgh	8 Everleth Dr.	(518) 561-0403
7	Microtel Inn Plattsburgh	554 NY 3	(518) 324-3800
8	Hampton Inn Plattsburgh	586 NY 3	(518) 324-1100
9	Fairfield Inn Plattsburgh	579 NY 3	(518) 536-7600

MAP 30 — ROUSES POINT

Hotels / Motels

1	Golden Gate Lodging	432 N Margaret St.	(518) 561-2040
2	Rip Van Winkle Motel	15 MacDonough Highway	(518) 324-4567

B&Bs / Inns

1	Point Au Roche Lodge	463 Point Au Roche Rd.	(518) 563-8714
2	Marine Village Cottages	82 Dickson Point Rd.	(518) 563-5698
3	B&B Au Bord du Lac	250 Lake St.	(518) 593-3432

CAMPGROUNDS

The listings below vary widely in regard to amenities and distance from the trail. Most DEC sites, for example, only offer primitive backcountry camping, whereas some private campgrounds include designated sites with access to showers and other facilities. Research camping options beforehand and plan route adjustments accordingly.

MAP 7 — MAHOPAC - CARMEL

Campgrounds

1	Nimham Mountain Multiple Use Area	Gipsy Trail Rd.	(845) 256-3076
2	Clarence Fahnestock State Park	NY 301	(845) 225-7207

MAP 9 — HOPEWELL JUNCTION

Campgrounds

1	Depot Hill Multiple Use Area	300 Depot Hill Rd.	(845) 256-3000
2	Sylvan Lake Beach Park	18 McDonnells Ln.	(845) 221-9889

MAP 11 — HIGHLAND - NEW PALTZ

Campgrounds

1	Mills Norrie State Park	9 Old Post Rd.	(845) 889-4646
2	Sam Pryor Shawanagunk Gateway	953 NY 299	(303) 951-4571
3	Yogi Bear's Jellystone Park	50 Bevier Rd.	(845) 255-5193

MAP 13 — KINGSTON

Campgrounds

1	Mills Norrie State Park	9 Old Post Rd.	(845) 889-4646

MAP 14 — TIVOLI - GERMANTOWN

Campgrounds

1	Brook n Wood Family Campground	1947 County Rte. 8	(518) 537-6896
2	Roe-Jan Kill Park	337 Dales Bridge Rd.	(518) 537-6687

MAP 15 — CATSKILL - HUDSON

Campgrounds

1	Roe-Jan Kill Park	337 Dales Bridge Rd.	(518) 537-6687
2	Lake Taghkanic State Park	1528 NY 82	(518) 851-3631
3	Livingston State Forest	51-55 Fox Creek Rd.	(518) 357-2155

MAP 16 — HUDSON - KINDERHOOK
Campgrounds
1	Schodack Island State Park	1 Schodack Island Way	(518) 732-0187

MAP 17 — VALATIE - NASSAU
Campgrounds
1	Schodack Island State Park	1 Schodack Island Way	(518) 732-0187

MAP 18 — EAST GREENBUSH - RENSSELAER
Campgrounds
1	Schodack Island State Park	1 Schodack Island Way	(518) 732-0187

MAP 20 — COHOES - WATERFORD
Campgrounds
1	Waterford Canal Visitor Center	1 Tugboat Alley	(518) 233-9123

MAP 21 — MECHANICVILLE - STILLWATER
Campgrounds
1	Lock C4 Stillwater	947 Stillwater Bridge Rd.	(518) 664-5261

MAP 23 — FORT EDWARD - HUDSON FALLS
Campgrounds
1	Moreau Lake State Park	605 Old Saratoga Rd.	(518) 793-0511

MAP 24 — FORT ANN
Campgrounds
1	Lock C9 Smith's Basin	2450 NY 149	(518) 747-6021

MAP 26 — TICONDEROGA
Campgrounds
1	Rogers Rock Campground	9894 Lake Shore Dr.	(518) 585-6746

MAP 27 — CROWN POINT - PORT HENRY
Campgrounds
1	Putnam Pond Campground	763 Putts Pond Rd.	(518) 585-7280
2	Crown Point Campground	784 Bridge Rd.	(518) 597-3603
3	Lincoln Pond Campground	4363 Lincoln Pond Rd.	(518) 942-5292
4	Barber Homestead Park	68 Barber Ln.	(518) 962-8989

MAP 29 — PLATTSBURGH
Campgrounds
1	Ausable Point Campground	3346 Lakeshore Dr.	(518) 561-7080
2	Ausable Chasm Campground	634 NY 373	(518) 834-9990
3	Ausable River Campground	367 NY 9N	(518) 834-9379

MAP 30 — ROUSES POINT
Campgrounds
1	Kings Bay Resort	1 Point Au Fer Rd.	(514) 972-2272
2	Cumberland Bay State Park	152 Cumberland Head Rd.	(518) 563-5240
3	Monty's Bay Campsites	715 Lake Shore Rd.	(518) 846-7342

BICYCLE SHOPS
Asterisk denotes rentals available

MAP 1 — LOWER MANHATTAN - GREENWICH VILLAGE
1	Waterfront Bicycle Shop*	391 West St., Manhattan	(212) 414-2453
2	Trek Bicycle Chelsea	183 Eighth St., Manhattan	(212) 255-5100
3	Sid's Bikes NYC	151 W 19th St., Manhattan	(212) 989-1060
4	Bicycle Habitat	228 Seventh Ave., Manhattan	(212) 206-6949

MAP 2 — MIDTOWN WEST - UPPER WEST SIDE
1	Enoch's Bike Shop*	480 Tenth Ave., Manhattan	(212) 582-0620
2	Trek Bicycle Hell's Kitchen	653 Tenth Ave., Manhattan	(212) 581-4500
3	Toga Bike Shop*	110 West End Ave., Manhattan	(212) 799-9625
4	Master Bike Shop*	265 W 72nd St., Manhattan	(212) 580-2355
5	Trek Bicycle Upper West Side	156 W 72nd St., Manhattan	(646) 868-5354

MAP 3 — WEST HARLEM
1	Trek Bicycle Upper West Side	231 W 96th St., Manhattan	(212) 663-7531
2	Champion Bicycles*	896 Amsterdam Ave., Manhattan	(212) 662-2690
3	Innovation Bike Shop*	105 W 106th St., Manhattan	(212) 678-7130
4	Larry's Freewheeling*	301 Cathedral Pkwy., Manhattan	(212) 280-7800
5	Junior Bicycle Shop	1826 Amsterdam Ave., Manhattan	(212) 690-6511

MAP 4 — BRONX - YONKERS
1	Manny's Bicycle	8 Bennett Ave., Manhattan	(212) 927-8501
2	Tread Bike Shop*	250 Dyckman St., Manhattan	(212) 544-7055
3	County Cycle Center	970 McLean Ave., Yonkers	(914) 237-8641
4	Garcia's Bicycle Shop	512 E 240th St., Bronx	(347) 341-5992
5	Bronx River Bicycle Works	27 Mt Vernon Ave., Mt Vernon	(914) 667-7417

MAP 5 — ARDSLEY - PLEASANTVILLE
1	Hastings Velo	45 Main St., Hastings-on-Hudson	(914) 478-2453
2	Endless Trail Bikeworx*	56 Main St., Dobbs Ferry	(914) 674-8567
3	Danny's Cycles*	644 Central Park Ave., Scarsdale	(914) 723-3408
4	Crank Cycles	14-16 N Central Ave., Hartsdale	(914) 461-0011
5	Sleek eBikes*	37 Main St., Tarrytown	(914) 909-1790
6	Ride of Pleasantville	351 Manville Rd., Pleasantville	(203) 433-2780

MAP 6 — BRIARCLIFF MANOR - YORKTOWN HEIGHTS
1	Briarcliff Bike Works	1250 Pleasantville Rd. Briarcliff Manor	(914) 762-7614
2	Julio Bicycles	45 Bedford Rd., Chappaqua	(914) 238-1312
3	Bicycle World NY	7 E Main St., Mt Kisco	(914) 666-4044
4	Yorktown Cycles*	1899 Commerce St., Yorktown Heights	(914) 245-5504

MAP 7 — MAHOPAC - CARMEL
1	Bikeway*	692 US 6, Mahopac	(845) 621-2800

MAP 8 — BREWSTER
1	Ski Haus	1611 NY 22, Brewster	(845) 279-3100
2	Pawling Cycle & Sport*	3198 NY 22, Patterson	(845) 878-7400

MAP 10 — POUGHKEEPSIE
1	Wheel & Heel	2658 E Main St., Wappingers Falls	(845) 632-3050
2	Bikeway*	1581 NY 376, Wappingers Falls	(845) 463-7433
3	Leisure Ride Bike*	266 Titusville Rd., Poughkeepsie	(845) 486-8125
4	pv Bicycle Shop	1557 Main St., Pleasant Valley	(845) 635-3161

MAP 10A — DOWNTOWN POUGHKEEPSIE
1	The Vintage Fixie	322 Main St., Poughkeepsie	(845) 489-7642

MAP 11A — DOWNTOWN NEW PALTZ
1	Bicycle Depot*	15 Main St., New Paltz	(845) 255-3859
2	The Bicycle Rack	13 N Front St., New Paltz	(845) 255-1770

MAP 12 — ROSENDALE
1	TRT Bicycles*	1066 NY 32, Rosendale	(845) 658-7832

MAP 12A — DOWNTOWN KINGSTON
1	Utility Bicycle Works	228 Wall St., Kingston	(845) 481-0269
2	Revolution Bicycles	388 Hasbrouck Ave., Kingston	(845) 853-8300

MAP 13 — KINGSTON
1	Kingston Cyclery	985 Morton Blvd., Kingston	(845) 382-2453
2	Bike Brothers	139 Boices Ln., Kingston	(845) 336-5581
3	Breakaway Cycles	6795 US 9, Rhinebeck	(845) 516-4849
4	Rhinebeck Bicycle Shop*	10 W Garden St., Rhinebeck	(845) 876-4025

MAP 15A — DOWNTOWN HUDSON
1	Steiner's Sports	301 Warren St., Hudson	(518) 828-5063

MAP 16 — KINDERHOOK - HUDSON
1	Velo Domestique	1006 Kinderhook St., Valatie	(518) 392-3010

MAP 17 — VALATIE - NASSAU
1	Steiner's Sports	3455 US 9, Valatie	(518) 784-3663

MAP 18A — DOWNTOWN ALBANY
1	Downtube Bicycle Works	466 Madison Ave., Albany	(518) 434-1711

MAP 19 — ALBANY - TROY
1	Steiner's Sports	329 Glenmont Rd., Glenmont	(518) 427-2406
2	Savile Road	257 Delaware Ave., Delmar	(518) 439-4766
3	The Freewheel	21A Railroad Ave., Albany	(541) 924-8879

MAP 20 — COHOES - WATERFORD
1	Troy Bike Rescue	3280 6th Ave., Troy	n/a
2	Elevate Cycles	215 Guideboard Rd., Clifton Park	(518) 371-4641

MAP 22A — SCHUYLERVILLE - HUDSON CROSSING PARK
1	Adirondack Ultra Cycling	160 Broad St., Schuylerville	(518) 583-3708

MAP 23 — FORT EDWARD - HUDSON FALLS
1	Evergreen Bicycle Works*	71 East St., Fort Edward	(518) 223-9921

MAP 23A — GLENS FALLS
1	Grey Ghost Bicycles*	76 Lawrence St., Glens Falls	(518) 223-0158

MAP 26 — TICONDEROGA
1	The Hub Bike Shop	27 Market St., Brant Lake	(518) 494-4822

MAP 28 — WESTPORT - WILLSBORO
1	LeepOff Cycles	23 Market St., Keene Valley	(518) 524-0212

MAP 29 — PLATTSBURGH
1	Viking Ski N' Cycle	770 NY 3, Plattsburgh	(518) 561-5539

MAP 29A — DOWNTOWN PLATTSBURGH
1	Maui North	31 Durkee St., Plattsburgh	(518) 563-7245

CRAFT BEVERAGES

MAP 1 — LOWER MANHATTAN - GREENWICH VILLAGE
1	Torch & Crown Brewing	12 Vandam St., Manhattan	(212) 228-7005
2	Great Jones Distilling	686 Broadway, Manhattan	(332) 910-9880
3	City Winery	25 11th Ave., Manhattan	(646) 751-6033
4	Our/NY Vodka Bar & Distillery	151 W 26th St., Manhattan	(646) 753-5556

MAP 2 — MIDTOWN WEST - UPPER WEST SIDE
1	Death Ave	315 10th Ave., Manhattan	(212) 695-8080

MAP 4 — BRONX - YONKERS
1	Gun Hill Brewing	3227 Laconia Ave., Bronx	(718) 881-0010
2	Yonkers Brewing	92 Main St., Yonkers	(914) 226-8327

MAP 5 — ARDSLEY - PLEASANTVILLE
1	Captain Lawrence Brewing	444 Saw Mill River Rd., Elmsford	(914) 741-2337
2	Prospero Winery	123 Castleton St., Pleasantville	(914) 769-6252
3	Soul Brewing	41 Wheeler Ave., Pleasantville	(914) 800-7685

MAP 6 — BRIARCLIFF MANOR - YORKTOWN HEIGHTS
1	Thompson's Cider Mill	335 Blinn Rd., Croton-on-Hudson	(914) 271-2254

MAP 7 — MAHOPAC - CARMEL
1	Kas Krupnikas	46 Miller Rd., Mahopac	(845) 750-6000

MAP 10 — POUGHKEEPSIE
1	Obercreek Brewing	59 Marlorville Rd., Wappingers Falls	(845) 632-1078
2	The Vale Fox Distillery	619 Noxon Rd., Poughkeepsie	(845) 210-9150
3	Plan Bee Farm Brewery	115 Underhill Rd., Poughkeepsie	(765) 307-8589

MAP 10A — DOWNTOWN POUGHKEEPSIE
1	Blue Collar Brewery	40 Cottage St., Poughkeepsie	(845) 454-2739
2	Mill House Brewing	289 Mill St., Poughkeepsie	(845) 485-2739
3	King's Court Brewing	40 Cannon St., Poughkeepsie	(917) 697-3030
4	Slate Point Meadery	184 Main St., Poughkeepsie	(845) 310-4220
	Zeus Brewing	178 Main St., Poughkeepsie	(845) 320-4560

MAP 11 — HIGHLAND - NEW PALTZ
1	Hudson Ale Works	17 Milton Ave., Highland	(845) 384-2531
2	Bad Seed Cider Farm Bar	341 Pancake Hollow Rd., Highland	(845) 236-0956
3	Brooklyn Cider House	155 N Ohioville Rd., New Paltz	(845) 633-8657
4	Kettleborough Cider House	277 NY 208, New Paltz	(845) 255-7717
5	Hyde Park Brewing	4076 Albany Post Rd., Hyde Park	(845) 229-8277

MAP 11A — DOWNTOWN NEW PALTZ
1	Clemson Bros. Brewery	3 Main St., New Paltz	(845) 256-1700
2	Coppersea Distilling	239 Springtown Rd., New Paltz	(845) 444-1044

MAP 12A — DOWNTOWN KINGSTON
1	Keegan Ales	20 St. James St., Kingston	(845) 331-2739
2	Kingston Standard Brewing	22 Jansen Ave., Kingston	(845) 853-8152
3	Hetta Glogg	85 Broadway, Kingston	(845) 216-4801

MAP 13 — KINGSTON
1 Great Life Brewing	75 Clarendon Ave., Kingston	(845) 331-3700

MAP 14 — TIVOLI - GERMANTOWN
1 Rose Hill Winery & Cidery	14 Rose Hill, Red Hook	(845) 758-4215
2 From The Ground Brewery	301 Guski Rd., Red Hook	(845) 309-8100
3 Clermont Vineyards & Winery	241 County Rte. 6, Germantown	(845) 663-6611
4 Tousey Winery	1774 US 9, Germantown	(518) 567-5462
Hudson Valley Distillers	1727 US 9, Germantown	(518) 537-6820

MAP 15 — CATSKILL - HUDSON
1 Crossroads Brewing	201 Water St., Catskill	(518) 291-4550
2 Subversive Brewing	96 W Bridge St., Catskill	(518) 303-1270
3 Crossroads Brewing	21 Second St. Athens	(518) 945-2337

MAP 15A — DOWNTOWN HUDSON
1 Hudson Brewing	99 S 3rd St., Hudson	(518) 697-5400

MAP 17 — VALATIE - NASSAU
1 Reifenberg Brewing	3021 Main St., Valatie	(518) 610-8447
2 Harvest Spirits	3074 US 9, Valatie	(518) 758-1776
3 S&S Farm Brewery	174 Middle Rd., Nassau	(518) 336-0766

MAP 18 — EAST GREENBUSH - RENSSELAER
1 Stable Gate Winery	12 Linda Way, Castleton	(518) 265-5133

MAP 18A — DOWNTOWN ALBANY
1 The Bull & Bee Meadery	140 Hamilton St., Albany	(518) 312-1053
2 CH Evans/Albany Pump Station	19 Quackenbush Sq., Albany	(518) 447-9000

MAP 19 — ALBANY - TROY
1 The Warbler Brewery	155 Delaware Ave., Delmar	(518) 650-8484
2 Albany Distilling	75 Livingston Ave., Albany	(518) 949-2472
3 Capital Distillery	32 Learned St., Albany	(518) 594-0175
Nine Pin Cider Works	929 Broadway, Albany	(518) 449-9999
4 Fort Orange Brewing	450 N Pearl St., Albany	(518) 992-3103
Druthers Brewing	1053 Broadway, Albany	(518) 650-7996

MAP 19A — DOWNTOWN TROY
1 Rare Form Brewing	90 Congress St., Troy	(518) 326-4303
2 Brown's Brewing	417 River St., Troy	(518) 273-2337

MAP 20 — COHOES - WATERFORD
1 Table 41 Brewing	188 Remsen St., Cohoes	(518) 414-2011
Bye-i Brewing	122 Remsen St., Cohoes	(518) 244-3924

MAP 22 — SCHUYLERVILLE
1 Victory View Vineyard	11975 NY 40, Schaghticoke	(518) 461-7132
2 Argyle Brewing	1 Main St., Greenwich	(518) 692-2585

MAP 22A — SCHUYLERVILLE - HUDSON CROSSING PARK
1 Bound by Fate Brewing	31 Ferry St., Schuylerville	(518) 507-6246
2 Saratoga Apple	1174 NY 29, Schuylerville	(518) 695-3131

MAP 23 — FORT EDWARD - HUDSON FALLS
1	Slickfin Brewing	147 Broadway, Fort Edward	(518) 223-0264

MAP 23A — GLENS FALLS
1	Glens Falls Distillery	18 Curran Ln., Glens Falls	(518) 502-1450
2	Cooper's Cave Ale	2 Sagamore St., Glens Falls	(518) 792-0007
3	Mean Max Brew Works	193 Glen St., Glens Falls	(518) 793-2337
4	Davidson Brothers Brewing	184 Glen St., Glens Falls	(518) 743-9026

MAP 24 — FORT ANN
1	Battle Hill Brewing	4 Charles St., Fort Ann	(518) 639-1033
2	Lake George Distilling	11262 NY 149, Fort Ann	(518) 639-1025

MAP 28 — WESTPORT - WILLSBORO
1	Ledge Hill Brewing	6700 Main St., Westport	(518) 962-2803
2	Boquet Valley Vineyard	25 Vineyard Way, Essex	(518) 570-6704
3	Highlands Vineyard	1092 Highland Rd., Keeseville	(518) 836-5355

MAP 29 — PLATTSBURGH
1	Ausable Brewing	765 Mace Chasm Rd., Keeseville	(518) 900-2739
2	Livingood's Brewery	697 Bear Swamp Rd., Peru	(518) 643-2020
3	Adirondack Ciderhouse	7411 US 9, Plattsburgh	(518) 563-2750

MAP 29A — DOWNTOWN PLATTSBURGH
1	Valcour Brewing	49 Ohio Ave., Plattsburgh	(518) 324-2337
2	OVAL Craft Brewing	111 Ohio Ave., Plattsburgh	(518) 324-2739

MAP 30 — ROUSES POINT
1	Vesco Ridge Vineyards	167 Stratton Hill Rd., W Chazy	(518) 846-8544
2	Amazing Grace Winery	9839 US 9, Chazy	(518) 215-4044
3	Four Maples Winery	40 Gamlaw Rd., Champlain	(518) 298-9463

Horsing around at the Waterford Harbor Visitors Center

CYCLING SAFETY

The following suggestions are for safe and enjoyable cycling, especially on the on-road sections of the route.

Wear a helmet
Cyclists are strongly encouraged to wear a helmet. Every year, bicycling accidents result in more sports-related head injuries than any other activity. While wearing a helmet does not prevent accidents, research shows that bicycle helmets can prevent three out of four serious cycling head injuries.

In New York State, riders ages 1-13 are required to wear an approved helmet. Children ages 1-4 must ride in a child seat. No children under the age of one are permitted on a bicycle.

Your helmet should sit flat atop your head, fit snugly, not obstruct visibility, and be approved by the Consumer Product Safety Commission (cpsc.org) or the Snell Memorial Foundation (smf.org).

Follow rules of the road
Cyclists in New York State have the same responsibilities as motorists and are required to follow all traffic regulations. Riders can make their trips safer by observing some basic traffic rules.
- Stop at red lights, obey all posted signs, and follow lane markings.
- Ride with traffic. Do not ride on sidewalks.
- When turning, use turn lanes and proper hand signals.
- Don't pass on the right. Cars and trucks have blind spots, especially in the right rear corner.
- Never wear headphones in both ears while cycling.

See and be seen
Cyclists are part of a complex traffic environment and cannot assume that motor vehicles will always yield to them. Be aware of your surroundings and make yourself visible to motorists.
- Always ride where approaching and passing motorists can see you.
- Wear bright-colored clothing during the day and reflective clothing or patches at night.
- Mount reflectors on wheels, pedals, and other surfaces.
- New York State law requires that bicyclists use both front and rear lights at night. The headlight should be visible from at least 500 feet and the taillight from 300 feet.
- Stay aware of surrounding traffic. Make eye contact with motorists and pedestrians at intersections and when merging.

Some additional cycling safety and comfort considerations
- Ride a bike that is the right size and correctly adjusted.
- Keep your bike in good repair. Check brakes and tires regularly.
- Watch out for hazards in the road. Avoid parallel-slat sewer grates, potholes, gravel, sand, ice, and debris.
- Dress appropriately. Layers allow you to adjust to temperature changes. In rain, wear a rain jacket or waterproof suit.
- On long trips and hot days, prevent dehydration by drinking plenty of fluids.

TRAIL ETIQUETTE

The Empire State Trail is a multi-use trail that is used for walking, hiking, jogging, cycling, in-line skating, cross-country skiing, and, where permitted, horseback riding and snowmobiling. Help make everyone's trail experience pleasant by following accepted trail etiquette.

- **Wheels yield to heels.** Cyclists stay to the right and yield the right of way to all other trail users.
- **Signal when passing.** Give a courteous audible warning when passing pedestrians and other bicyclists.
- **Maintain control of your speed.** Approach turns by anticipating someone around the bend. Be able to stop safely within the distance you can see down the trail.
- **Don't block the trail.** When in a group, use no more than half the trail, so as not to block the flow of other users.
- **Stay on the trail.** Avoid trespassing on private land and trampling vegetation. Work is ongoing to improve and expand existing trails; respect trail and road closure and detour signs.
- **Do not disturb wildlife or livestock.** Avoid sudden movements, loud noises, and unexpected approaches that can startle animals and be dangerous to cyclists.
- **Leave No Trace.** Carry out what you carry in.
- **Be respectful.** Be respectful of other trail users regardless of their speed or skill level.
- **Follow all posted regulations.** Many different state, county, and municipal agencies manage segments of the Empire State Trail; their rules and regulations sometimes differ.
- **Be cautious at intersections.** Pedestrians and dismounted cyclists have the right of way at all road/trail intersections marked with a crosswalk, but always use caution when crossing intersections.
- **Follow e-bike regulations.** As e-bikes become more popular and see more use along the trail, e-bike users need to be respectful of other trail users. Follow all posted speed limits, use caution, and do not ride on sections that prohibit the use of e-bikes. E-bike users should yield to all other trail users, including those riding traditional bicycles.

TRAVEL AND LOGISTICS

Travel options abound along the Empire State Trail corridor.
Following are a few ideas to help you plan your trip.

Distances
You're never very far from "civilization" on the Empire State Trail.

The following chart provides distances between some of the larger
communities along the route.

	NYC/The Battery	Elmsford	Brewster	Hopewell Junction	Poughkeepsie	New Paltz	Kingston	Hudson	Kinderhook	Albany	Waterford	Schuylerville	Fort Edward	Whitehall	Ticonderoga	Westport	Plattsburgh	Rouses Point/Canadian Border
NYC/The Battery		29	65	89	102	111	131	166	177	201	212	237	252	277	301	328	373	400
Elmsford	29		36	60	74	82	102	137	148	172	183	208	223	248	272	299	344	371
Brewster	65	36		24	38	47	66	101	112	136	147	172	187	212	236	263	308	335
Hopewell Junction	89	60	24		14	23	42	77	88	112	123	148	163	188	212	239	284	311
Poughkeepsie	102	74	38	14		9	29	64	75	99	110	135	150	175	199	226	271	298
New Paltz	111	82	47	23	9		20	55	66	90	101	126	141	166	190	217	262	289
Kingston	131	102	66	42	29	20		35	46	70	81	106	121	146	170	197	242	269
Hudson	166	137	101	77	64	55	35		11	35	46	71	86	111	135	162	207	234
Kinderhook	177	148	112	88	75	66	46	11		24	35	60	75	100	124	151	196	223
Albany	201	172	136	112	99	90	70	35	24		11	36	51	76	100	127	172	199
Waterford	212	183	147	123	110	101	81	46	35	11		25	40	65	89	116	161	188
Schuylerville	237	208	172	148	135	126	106	71	60	36	25		15	40	64	91	136	163
Fort Edward	252	223	187	163	150	141	121	86	75	51	40	15		25	49	76	121	148
Whitehall	277	248	212	188	175	166	146	111	100	76	65	40	25		24	51	96	123
Ticonderoga	301	272	236	212	199	190	170	135	124	100	89	64	49	24		27	72	99
Westport	328	299	263	239	226	217	197	162	151	127	116	91	76	51	27		45	72
Plattsburgh	373	344	308	284	271	262	242	207	196	172	161	136	121	96	72	45		27
Rouses Point/Canadian Border	400	371	335	311	298	289	269	234	223	199	188	163	148	123	99	72	27	

Views of the Catskills from Olana State Historic Site

Renting a bike

For spur of the moment trips in which you just want a taste of cycling along the Empire State Trail, renting a bicycle is a good option. The bike shop listings in this guide indicate which shops offer rentals.

Transporting your bike

The north-south corridor of the Empire State Trail offers four main travel modes: air, rail, bus, and car. Unless you rent a bike locally, the first three of these require that you make special preparations to travel with your bicycle. Usually, this means breaking down your bicycle so that it will fit into a standard bike-shipping box (available at most bicycle and shipping stores). Preparing a bicycle for a shipping box typically entails removing the pedals and re-attaching them on the inside of the crankshaft and turning the handlebar so it is parallel with the wheel. If you are willing to spend a few extra dollars, consider shipping your bicycle directly to your first night's lodging. If you aren't comfortable breaking down and re-assembling your bicycle, inquire if, for a fee, it can be shipped from a bike shop near you to a bike shop near your starting point. To ship on your own, visit bikeflights.com or check with UPS (1-800-742-5877) for shipping costs. Shipping takes two to eight days depending upon the distance. To be safe, we recommend that you ship your bike at least seven days in advance.

UPS shipping requirements
- Maximum weight is 150 pounds
- Maximum measurements are 165 inches, length and girth combined
- Maximum length is 108 inches
- UPS recommends placing 2-4 inches of packing material around your bike to protect it. Tape an address label inside your box and attach an address label on each side of the outside of the box.

Plane

Major airports in New York City connect with Albany frequently, and make air travel in the southern half of the Empire State Trail easy to plan. While Plattsburgh does have an airport, flights do not often connect to Albany or New York City. Bear in mind that commercial airlines usually charge an extra fee to transport bicycles. If two one-way flights are too expensive or not allowed from your embarkation location, consider flying round-trip to your starting location and using train or bus transportation to travel back to your starting point.

Train

Amtrak is another option for Empire State Trail riders. Many Amtrak stations serve the Hudson River Corridor: New York - Penn Station, Yonkers, Croton-Harmon, Poughkeepsie, Rhinecliff, Hudson, Albany-Rensselaer, Saratoga Springs, Fort Edward, Whitehall, Ticonderoga, Port Henry, Westport, Port Kent, Plattsburgh, and Rouses Point. However, as of the publication of this guide, the Adirondack service between New York City and Montreal, that provides the only service for stations from Whitehall north, is suspended due to the COVID-19 pandemic. It is unknown when service will resume.

Certain Amtrak routes in New York State, including the Empire Service between New York City and Albany and the Ethan Allen Express from New York City to Fort Edward (and beyond to points in Vermont) allow "carry-on" bicycle service, allowing train riders to carry their bike directly onto passenger cars. The Adirondack may also offer carry-on bicycle service when service on that route resumes. Check amtrak.com for more information.

Amtrak requires a bicycle reservation and charges a $20 fee to reserve the space on these routes. A limited number of bicycles are allowed on any given train. To transport a bike in these cars, the front wheel and any panniers or bags must be removed. Carry-on bicycle service is restricted to standard-size bicycles up to 50 lbs., with a maximum allowed tire width of 2 inches.

All Amtrak trains allow foldable bicycles on board in lieu of a piece of carry-on luggage, space permitting. Folding bicycles must be no greater than 34 in x. 15 in. x 48 in. when folded. Folding bicycles are not allowed in overhead storage bins; they must be stored in the luggage areas at either end of the car.

Bicycles can be transported in boxes if specific bicycle space is sold out, if you are changing trains, or if you are shipping a tandem, recumbent, cargo bike or fat tire bicycle. Bicycles can also be shipped independently using Amtrak Express.

Call 1-800-872-7245 or visit amtrak.com for more information.

For those traveling between New York City and Poughkeepsie, Metro-North train service is also available. Metro-North stations closest to the Empire State Trail are on the Hudson Line. Stations include Grand Central Terminal, many stops in Manhattan and the Bronx, Yonkers, Hastings-on-Hudson, Dobbs Ferry, Ardsley-on-

Hudson, Irvington, Tarrytown, Ossining, Croton-Harmon, Cortlandt, Peekskill, Garrison, Cold Spring, Fishkill, Beacon, New Hamburg, and Poughkeepsie.

Riders no longer need a permit to bring a bicycle on Metro-North trains, though there are rules to follow regarding transport. All bicycles carried on board must be clean and free of excessive dirt and grease. Cyclists may board trains only after all other customers have boarded, and must remain in the immediate proximity of and in full control of their bicycles at all times. Only single-seat, human-powered, two-wheeled vehicles, with a wheel diameter not in excess of 27 inches and maximum dimensions of 80"x 48" are allowed. Bicycles in excess of the above dimensions, as well as tandem, motorized, or training-wheeled bicycles, tricycles, or bicycles with any protrusions that could cause injury or damage are not permitted. Folding bicycles are allowed, and must remain folded at all times.

Bicycles can also be transported on Metro-North's Harlem Line from Grand Central Terminal through the Bronx to Brewster, which has a station near the Empire State Trail.

Automobile

If you're coming from a relatively short distance, the most convenient way to access the Empire State Trail may be by car. For those not traveling solo, using two vehicles offers several options. The simplest option is to drop one vehicle at your planned destination, then drive, with your bikes and luggage, in the other car to your starting point. At the end of your trip, drive back to retrieve the other car. This approach works for both single- and multi-day trips. Remember to keep both sets of keys with you! If you're planning to travel the entire length of the trail, however, this method means a long drive to retrieve the second car at the end of your trip. Another option is to send one or two people back to the first car via Amtrak or Metro-North (the rest of the group should treat them to dinner when they return) while everyone else enjoys a day exploring the local area. This works particularly well if you park the first car at an Amtrak or Metro-North station.

A more complex variation of the car-drop approach for a multi-day trip is to take two cars, but instead of dropping one car at your ultimate destination, drop it at each day's end point. At the end of a day's riding, drive back to where the first car is parked, drive both cars to the day's end point, then drive one car out to the next day's destination. The benefits of this car-hopping method are that you always have a car with you in the evening, you can use day-use parking areas, and your second car is close by at the end of your trip.

The downside is that you must spend hours each day driving. When dropping off cars as part of a multi-day trip, park at well-used, secure locations, such as an Amtrak station or a parking lot with long-term rates. If you're starting or ending your journey at a hotel, motel, or B&B, you might inquire if you can park your car there.

Solo travelers and groups with only one car can combine driving with return trips on the bus or train. A convenient arrangement is to drive to your starting point and park at an Amtrak station. Ride the trail to another community with an Amtrak station. Store your bicycle in a secure spot (such as your room, if you're staying in a motel or B&B). Take the train back to your car and drive back to where your bike is stored.

The ideal scenario for cyclists is to have a support or 'sag' vehicle shadowing them as a backup for food, equipment, and emergencies. If you have a non-cycling travel partner or members of your group willing to rotate in the support role, they can drive the vehicle while others bicycle.

Bus
Several bus companies serve the Hudson River corridor, but bus service is far less frequent and runs to fewer communities than Amtrak. Greyhound (greyhound.com) and Trailways (trailways.com) have the widest-ranging routes.

Megabus (megabus.com) and GotoBus (GotoBus.com) offer affordable, frequent service between New York City and Albany (Rensselaer Rail Station). Peter Pan (peterpanbus.com) offers connections between Albany and points east. Policies regarding transporting bikes on buses vary by vendor, so you should call ahead.

Car rental
Renting a car is an option. However, rental companies may not allow bike racks to be mounted on their vehicles. If you do rent a car, ask for a model with back seats that fold down so you can expand the trunk room to accommodate bicycles. If you can transport your bike in a rental car, getting a one-way rental at your final destination and driving to your starting point is an option.

Baggage shuttle
For those who plan to travel from one B&B to the next, and who like to travel light, call ahead to see if you can arrange for your luggage to be shuttled between destinations. That way, you only need to carry what you require for the day — rain jacket, tool kit, first-aid kit, food, water, camera, and other accessories.

Fully-supported ride

Parks & Trails New York is planning to host a fully-supported cycling trip in the Hudson Valley along the Empire State Trail in summer 2023, and we expect that the ride will be an annual event. Visit ptny.org for more information on our *Cycle the Hudson Valley* bike tour.

Border crossing

For those intending to cross the Canada border by bicycle, visit travel.gc.ca for more information. Plan well in advance in order to avoid surprises during international travel.

PREPARING FOR MULTI-DAY CYCLING TRIPS

Conditioning

Attaining a basic fitness level and comfort in the saddle before starting out will make your trip more enjoyable. Begin your preparations several weeks ahead of time and build slowly, especially if you haven't cycled in a while. It is always a good idea to consult with your physician before starting any exercise program.

Some training is better than none. Set a reasonable goal, given your schedule, and stick to it. Start with five-mile bike rides and, when you're comfortable, increase to 10-mile rides. If you'd like to prepare for multi-day and/or longer trips, continue adding five-mile increments until you are in the 30-mile range. Then, test your endurance by doing a 40- or 50-mile ride. Take rides with loaded racks or panniers to get accustomed to the extra weight and change in balance. By the time you start your trip, you should be comfortable spending at least four hours at a time in the saddle.

Get to know your body's food and hydration needs during long rides so that you can prepare for them in advance. If you plan to take children, it's essential to include them in the training plan. Use training trips to teach children to drink plenty of water, to eat regularly, and to follow the rules of the road and trail. Spend time honing their skills (and yours) riding in traffic. If you plan to carry small children in trailers or bike seats, use conditioning rides to test their comfort and endurance.

You might find it helpful to seek out a local cycling club for training advice and for opportunities to participate in group rides. You'll not only pick up many riding and equipment tips but you'll meet some great people who share your interest in cycling.

Equipment
Having the right equipment and gear makes a big difference.
Following are some basic equipment suggestions.

Bicycle
Your bicycle is the most critical piece of equipment for cycling
the Empire State Trail. Therefore, it's essential that it be both
comfortable and reliable. Newer, higher-end bikes tend to be lighter
and easier to ride, but older bicycles can certainly do the job. A wide
selection of gears will help reduce fatigue. New or old, make sure
your bike is in top mechanical condition and properly fitted and
adjusted to you. Most bike shops can perform a detailed inspection
and tune-up, as well as adjust your bike for proper fit. Many riders
use hybrid bikes because of their comfort and versatility, but gravel,
mountain, road, and touring bikes are also good options for the
Empire State Trail. Tandems, recumbents, and trikes are popular
options, too.

Keep in mind that you may be riding both on stone dust and paved
surfaces, so it is important to think about your tires. Tires with
puncture protection, and sized 28-42mm wide for 700c wheels and
1.3-1.6" wide for 26" wheels are recommended. If you ride a "skinny-
tire" road bike, using the widest tires the frame will accommodate
will provide a smoother ride. If you ride a mountain bike, non-
aggressive tires or "slicks" will reduce rolling resistance and make you
more efficient over long distances. You might also consider a folding
bicycle as it facilitates easy transport to the trail. Consult your local
bicycle shop for options.

Even if you are traveling light, without camping gear or overnight
baggage, you will still find some sort of handlebar bag or pannier
convenient to carry extra clothes, snacks, and other accessories. Small
backpacks or fanny packs can also serve in this capacity. Panniers
should attach securely to your bicycle frame to avoid weight shifting
and interference with your chain or wheels. Since you will most likely
stop often at points of interest, shops, and restaurants along the
route, take a sturdy bike lock. An easily detachable gear bag allows
you to take valuable items with you when you leave your bike.

As it's important to stay hydrated during a cycling trip, have at least
two water bottle cages or holders attached to your bike frame or
use a handlebar bag or panniers that can carry several water bottles.
A camelback water container, which is worn like a backpack, is also
an option.

Electric bicycles

Electric bicycles (e-bikes) have become an increasingly popular option for those looking for an easier way to travel on two wheels. As of this guide's publication in 2022, electric bicycles have only been legal in the state for two years, and the infrastructure and legal regulations to support them are new and likely to change greatly over the next five years.

Current New York State law governing e-bikes is somewhat complicated. Decisions on whether to allow Class 1 and Class 2 e-bikes on trails are set by the state or local government entity that owns a particular off-road trail section. Rules regarding the Empire State Trail are evolving. The NYS Canal Corporation, which administers sections of the Champlain Canalway Trail between Albany and Whitehall, allows Class 1 and 2 e-bikes. In addition, Class 1 and 2 e-bikes are allowed on the Albany-Hudson Electric Trail section of the EST in Rensselaer and Columbia Counties. To date, the only off-road Empire State Trail section where e-bikes are explicitly prohibited is in Manhattan and the Bronx (e-bikes are prohibited on bicycle trails in New York City). In addition, while Class 1 "pedal assist" e-bikes are allowed on the Wallkill Valley Rail Trail section from New Paltz to Kingston in Ulster County, Class 2 e-bikes are prohibited on the WVRT trail. The remainder of the Empire State Trail is administered by counties and local governments which own specific sections (e.g. the Westchester County Trail, Dutchess Rail Trail, etc.). To date most have not adopted formal policies, meaning e-bikes are neither explicitly allowed nor prohibited on those trail sections.

The availability of charging infrastructure along the trail varies from section to section. Public parks or marinas may have electrical hookups or charging stations that can be used; check with the site manager before using any outlets. The most reliable option will generally be to charge overnight at the hotel or bed & breakfast you're staying at for the following day's ride.

Clothing

To stay comfortable during a long cycling trip, your clothing must perform three functions: keep you dry, block wind, and cushion pressure points (hands and posterior). Your body controls its temperature through perspiration. Therefore, clothing that allows perspiration to easily evaporate will keep you dry and cool on hot days and dry and warm on cold days. Generally, cotton does this poorly because it absorbs and holds a lot of moisture. Modern synthetic fibers help 'wick' moisture away from skin to a garment's exterior. Clothing made from synthetic materials also dries quickly so you can wash it at night in a sink and usually wear it the next day. Most bicycle jerseys and shorts are made from synthetic materials, allowing the breeze you generate to sweep away your perspiration and keep you cool in warmer temperatures. Wool and wool blends used by some cycling and outdoor apparel manufacturers also promote wicking and dry quickly.

In cooler temperatures, the breeze from riding becomes an undesirable wind chill, forcing your body to strain to generate enough heat for your muscles to function efficiently. To compensate, add bulk through additional clothing layers or add a windproof shell or both. In very cool temperatures, it's also advisable to wear cycling tights or windproof pants. Invest in synthetic undergarments to take full advantage of the wicking phenomenon.

Layering allows you to adjust to a range of conditions. Remember that it can cool down significantly at night in upstate New York, especially in the spring and fall.

Rain will lower your body temperature even more quickly than wind so a good rain jacket is critical. Rain pants are also a good idea. Rain ponchos are not as good as jackets because they tend to billow while riding. In a pinch, a garbage bag with holes cut out for arms and head can help protect your body's core.

Water-resistant is not the same as waterproof. Water-resistant jackets will soak through in an extended rainstorm. Higher-end rain jackets use a waterproof and breathable coating that allows your perspiration to evaporate. Waterproof jackets and pants are also usually windproof so they can double as wind protection.

As you ride, the entire weight of your body presses onto your bike in three areas of contact: hands, feet, and posterior. Padded bicycle gloves help ease hand pressure and chafing as well as absorb vibrations from the front tire. Synthetic cycling socks can ease the pressure on the balls of your feet while pedaling. Using an additional thin liner sock can further keep your feet dry and reduce blisters. Many cyclists use special bicycle shoes, but the stiffer clip-in varieties can be inconvenient to walk in as you stop and visit the attractions and communities along the trail. If you do opt for a bicycle shoe, sneaker-type models with recessed cleats will allow you to more comfortably walk longer distances. Padded Lycra bicycling shorts are a must for longer trips. If you feel awkward about their appearance, you can wear a loose-fitting pair of regular shorts over them or purchase special bike touring shorts that have the appearance of normal shorts but are constructed with a pad.

Basic bike tool kit

Many bicycle tool kits are commercially available, but you can easily assemble your own. Essential tool kit ingredients:

- Spare tube, tube patch kit, tire lever
- Small frame pump
- Open end wrenches
- Allen wrenches
- Screwdrivers
- Chain tool, chain lube, extra chain links
- Small pliers / multi-purpose tool
- Zip ties or bailing wire
- Bungee cords
- Duct tape

First aid & emergency kit

The benefits of carrying a small first aid kit far outweigh the disadvantage of a little extra weight. Basic first aid kit ingredients:

- Bandages (assorted sizes, including triangular)
- Adhesive tape
- Antiseptic ointment
- Gauze pads and roller gauze (assorted sizes)
- Scissors and tweezers
- Small flashlight and extra batteries
- Swiss army knife or small folding knife
- Matches and candle

Other useful accessories

- Cell phone
- Sunglasses
- Camera
- Pad & pen
- Sunscreen
- Insect repellant

ADDITIONAL READING AND RESOURCES

A History of Native American Land Rights in Upstate New York by Cindy Amrhein—The History Press, 2016

Gotham: A History of New York City to 1898 by Edwin Burrows and Mike Wallace—Oxford University Press, 2000

Lake Champlain's Sailing Canal Boats: An Illustrated Journey from Burlington Bay to the Hudson River by Arthur B. Cohn—Lake Champlain Maritime Museum, 2003

An Indigenous Peoples' History of the United States by Roxanne Dunbar-Ortiz—Beacon Press 2015

The Hudson: America's River by Frances Dunwell—Columbia University Press, 2008

The Hudson River School: Nature and the American Vision by Linda Ferber and the New-York Historical Society—Rizzoli Electa, 2009

The Hudson Valley: The First 250 Million Years by David Levine—Globe Pequot Press, 2020

Historic Houses of the Hudson River Valley by Gregory Long, Bret Morgan, and James Ivory—Rizzoli, 2004

Albany: Capital City on the Hudson by John J. McEneny—American Historical Press, 1998

Wandering Home: A Long Walk Across America's Most Hopeful Landscape: Vermont's Champlain Valley and New York's Adirondacks by Bill McKibben—St. Martin's Griffin, 2014

Troy Through Time by Don Rittner – America Through Time, 2017

The Women Who Made New York by Julie Scelfo and Hallie Heald—Seal Press, 2016

North Star Country: Upstate New York and the Crusade for African American Freedom by Milton Sernett—Syracuse University Press, 2001

The Catskills: Its History and How It Changed America by Stephen M. Silverman, Raphael D. Silver—Knopf, 2015

The Nature of New York: An Environmental History of the Empire State by David Stradling—Cornell University Press, 2010

The Encyclopedia of New York by The Editors of New York Magazine – Avid Reader Press, 2020

Greater Gotham: A History of New York City from 1898 to 1919 by Mike Wallace—Oxford University Press, 2017

Lake Champlain: A Natural History by Mike Winslow, Glenn Novak, and Libby Walker Davidson—Images from the Past, 2008

At Lake Between: The Great Council Fire and the European Discovery of Lake Champlain by Frederick M Wiseman—Lake Champlain Maritime Museum, 2009

Rail-Trails: New Jersey & New York by Rails-to-Trails Conservancy—Wilderness Press, 2019

Children's Books

River by Elisha Cooper—Orchard Books, 2019

The Champlain Monster by Jeff Danziger—Green Writers Press, 2019

Her Right Foot by Dave Eggers and Shawn Harris—Chronicle Books, 2017

Jackson and Auggie: Adventure in the Hudson Valley by Renee Pearce and Kaylin Ruffino—Strategic Book Publishing, 2012

The Little Red Lighthouse and the Great Gray Bridge by Hildegarde H. Swift and Lynd Ward—HMH Books for Young Readers, 2002

River of Dreams: The Story of the Hudson River by Hudson Talbott—G.P. Putnam's Sons Books for Young Readers, 2009

Hello, Adirondacks! by Martha Zschock—Commonwealth Editions, 2013

ACKNOWLEDGEMENTS

Cycling the Hudson and Champlain Valleys was made possible through the contributions of many individuals and organizations. We sincerely thank them all.

Parks & Trails New York staff members who played a key role in this edition of the guidebook: **Rachel Carter, Dylan Carey, Robin Dropkin, Margaret McGivern, Erica Schneider,** and **Linden Horvath.**

Steve Spindler, of Steve Spindler Cartography, for the beautiful original maps. **Kelly Fahey**, of Primeau-Fahey Studios, for her high-quality graphic design. **Andy Beers** and **Scott Keller,** of the Hudson River Valley Greenway, for their careful edits and guidance.

The following tourism organizations were helpful in providing regional information: **Visit Westchester, Putnam County Tourism, Dutchess Tourism, Ulster County Alive, Columbia County Tourism, Rensselaer County Tourism,** and ROOST ADK.

PHOTOS COURTESY OF:

A special thank you to the NYS Office of Parks, Recreation & Historic Preservation for the beautiful cover photo of the Rosendale Trestle.

Crailo State Historic Site - Page 69; City of Troy - Page 79; David Mark - Pages 25, 31; Dutchess County Tourism - Pages 2, 57, 59; Dylan Carey - Pages 47, 77; Erica Schneider - Pages 93, 95, 127; Franklin D. Roosevelt Presidential Library and Museum - Page 41; Gary Yost - Page 11; Gerald Berliner - Page 51; Harry Gillen - Page 85; Hudson River Valley Greenway - Pages 21, 27, 33, 37, 49, 65, 67, 72, 73, Back Cover; Jimmy Woo - Page 41; Library of Congress - Pages 27, 35; Marcelo Lavin - Page 23; Matthew Kierstead - Page 53; The Metropolitan Museum of Art - Page 89; National Park Service - Pages 23, 83; New York Public Library - Page 85; NYS Office of Parks, Recreation & Historic Preservation - Cover Photo, Pages 8, 10, 20, 46, 87, 100, 101, 113; Pepe Productions - Page 91; Putnam County Tourism - Page 37; Rachel Carter - Pages 35, 39, 57, 59, 61, 63, 65, 81, 87, 89, 95, 99, 103, 105, 107, 109, 111, 113, 130, 142; Roger Lipera - Page 69; Rosendale Library - Page 53; S. Danzger - Page 29; Troy Savings Bank Music Hall - Page 79; Ulster County Tourism - Pages 49, 51, 55; Walkway Over the Hudson - Pages 3, 43.

GUIDEBOOK PARTNERS

PARKS & TRAILS NEW YORK

Parks & Trails New York is New York's leading statewide advocate for parks and trails, dedicated since 1985 to improving our health, economy, and quality of life through the use and enjoyment of green space. With thousands of members and  supporters across the state, PTNY is a leading voice in the protection of New York's magnificent state park system and the creation and promotion of more than 1,500 miles of greenways, bike paths, river walks, and trails. Visit ptny.org or call (518) 434-1583 for more information or to sign up for PTNY eNews.

MAURICE D. HINCHEY HUDSON RIVER VALLEY NATIONAL HERITAGE AREA (FEDERAL FUNDS)

The Maurice D. Hinchey Hudson River Valley National Heritage Area was designated by Congress in 1996 as the Hudson River Valley National Heritage Area and was officially renamed in honor 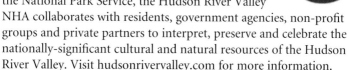 of Maurice D. Hinchey in 2019. In partnership with the National Park Service, the Hudson River Valley NHA collaborates with residents, government agencies, non-profit groups and private partners to interpret, preserve and celebrate the nationally-significant cultural and natural resources of the Hudson River Valley. Visit hudsonrivervalley.com for more information.

The views and conclusions contained in this document are those of the authors and should not be interpreted as representing the opinions or policies of the U.S. Government. Mention of trade names or commercial products does not constitute their endorsement by the U.S. Government.

View of the Essex Ferry on Lake Champlain

HUDSON RIVER VALLEY GREENWAY

The Hudson River Valley
Greenway advances the
state's commitment to the
preservation, enhancement,

and development of the world-renowned scenic, natural, historic,
cultural, and recreational resources of the Hudson River Valley,
while continuing to emphasize economic development activities and
remaining consistent with the tradition of municipal home rule.
The Greenway also manages the Hudson River Valley National
Heritage Area. Visit hudsongreenway.ny.gov to learn more about
the Greenway.

NORTHERN BORDER REGIONAL COMMISSION

The Northern Border Regional
Commission is a federal-state
partnership for economic and
community development in

northern Maine, New Hampshire, Vermont, and New York. Each
year, the NBRC provides federal funds for critical economic and
community development projects throughout the northeast. These
investments lead to new jobs being created and leverage substantial
private sector investments.

*This guidebook was funded by a grant from the Northern Border
Regional Commission. Support for this publication was made possible
in part with a Rural Business Development Grant from USDA Rural
Development.*

NEW YORK STATE OFFICE OF PARKS, RECREATION, AND HISTORIC PRESERVATION

The New York State
Office of Parks,
Recreation and
Historic Preservation

(State Parks) manages and protects the state's system of state
parks and historic sites, and also is charged with coordinating
and developing a statewide trails plan. These resources offer New
Yorkers opportunities to escape the daily grind, explore their natural
environment, and experience the state's rich cultural heritage.
For more information about State Parks, visit parks.ny.gov.

Your adventures. Reimagined.

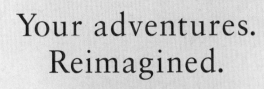

In Westchester County, the great outdoors is truly yours to explore. Enjoy more than 45 miles of picturesque cycling trails nestled among nearly 50,000 acres of accessible open space, including 18,000 acres of Westchester County parkland. Plan your next experience at **visitwestchesterny.com**.

visit
Westchester
County ny

Beyond expectations

North County Trailway

A ROUTE FOR EVERY RIDER.

Dutchess County offers the perfect path for every type of cyclist. From breathtaking views to idyllic country roads, you'll get lost in the beautiful scenery of Dutchess County at a pace that's all your own. Plan your bike trip at **dutchesstourism.com.**

Walkway Over the Hudson, Poughkeepsie, NY

PLAN
YOUR RIDE

A Storied
Experience.

bike
columbia county

For info on biking visit
bikecoco.com

BIKE COCO
BICYCLE
COLUMBIA
COUNTY
NEW YORK

For everything going on in Columbia County visit
columbiacountytourism.org

Columbia County Tourism

NEW YORK

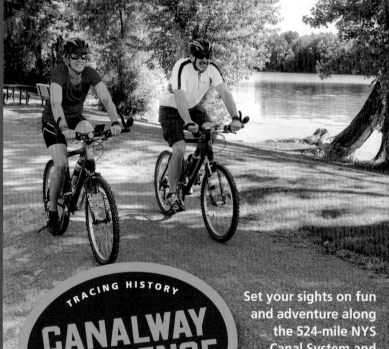

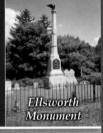